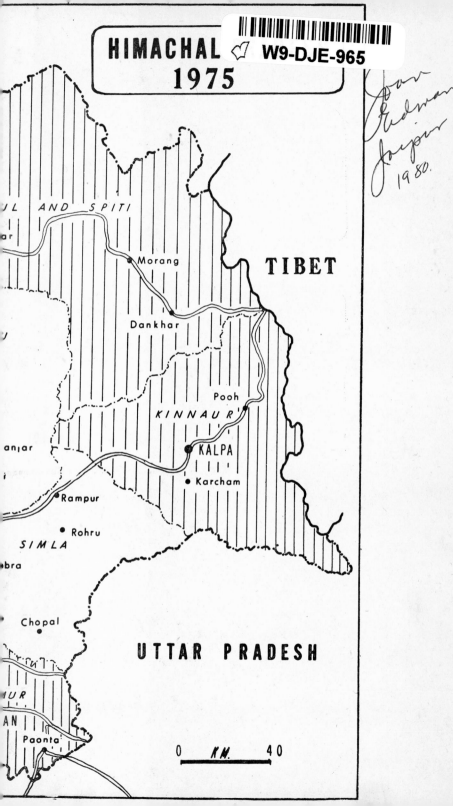

HIMACHAL
1975

TIBET

UTTAR PRADESH

KINNAUR

Morang

Dankhar

Pooh

KALPA

Karcham

Rampur

Rohru

SIMLA

Chopal

Paonta

L AND SPITI

anjar

bra

0   KM.   40

POLYANDRY IN THE HIMALAYAS

BY THE SAME AUTHOR

Himachal: Its Proper Shape and Status
Himachal Pradesh: Case for Statehood
Himachal Pradesh: Area and Language
Strategy for Development of Hill Areas

POLYANDRY
IN THE
HIMALAYAS

Y. S. PARMAR

VIKAS PUBLISHING HOUSE PVT LTD
DELHI   BOMBAY   BANGALORE   KANPUR

VIKAS PUBLISHING HOUSE PVT LTD
5 Daryaganj, Ansari Road, Delhi 110006
Savoy Chambers, 5 Wallace Street, Bombay 400001
10 First Main Road, Gandhi Nagar, Bangalore 560009
80 Canning Road, Kanpur 208004

COPYRIGHT © Y. S. PARMAR, 1975

First published, January 1975

Reprint, February 1975

ISBN 0 7069 0354 4

*Exclusive Distributors in UK, Europe, Middle East,
Africa, Australia, and New Zealand*
INTERNATIONAL BOOK DISTRIBUTORS LIMITED
66 Wood Lane End, Hemel Hempstead, Herts, England

PRINTED IN INDIA
AT INDIA OFFSET PRESS, NEW DELHI, AND PUBLISHED BY
MRS SHARDA CHAWLA, VIKAS PUBLISHING HOUSE
PVT LTD, 5 DARYAGANJ, ANSARI ROAD, DELHI-6

*To the hardworking
long suffering woman of the
Himalayas*

ACKNOWLEDGMENT

I acknowledge my debt of gratitude to the late Dr D.N. Majumdar of Canning College, Lucknow University, who inspired me to undertake research on the peculiar marriage institutions in the Himalayas and without whose guidance and help I could not have completed it. Nor can I forget the influence of that prolific writer and economist-cum-sociologist, the late Dr Radhakamal Mukerjee, my Professor and Head of the Department of Economics and Sociology, whose tireless habit of reading and writing left an indelible mark on my mind.

I acknowledge with thanks the help rendered by the late Colonel Kanwar Shiv Raj Singh, Naib-Dewan of the then Baroda State, for arranging some rare books on sociology from Baroda State Library. I am grateful to my late brother, Shri J.S. Parmar, Bar-at-Law, who did the original typing of the manuscript and to Shri R.C. Kaushesh, Private Secretary, for getting the final manuscript typed. Nor can I forget Shri B.S. Singh of the Indian Administrative Service for arranging the publication nor Dr Dube, Director of the Indian Institute of Advanced Study, Simla, for writing the Introduction. I owe a deep sense of gratitude to the Prime Minister, Shrimati Indira Gandhi, who has been gracious enough to write a foreword to the book.

FOREWORD

Himachal Pradesh is one of the most picturesque regions of India. But like our other hill areas, it has suffered greatly for lack of communications, which has kept the communities isolated and changes have been slower.

However in Himachal, as elsewhere, the old order is changing. Under the conforming pressures of modern life, its peculiar regional practices are being abandoned. Hence it is important for social anthropologists to make a careful analysis of various aspects of society in transition in order to help in psychological adjustment as well as for a correct historical assessment of the causes and consequences of the changes.

Dr Y.S. Parmar's book is a commendable effort in this direction. Polyandry is the subject of much ill-informed comment. Dr Parmar has rightly pointed out that there is usually some economic reason for a social custom and that without a change in economic motivation, no material and permanent change is possible. By putting it in its proper historical and economic context, the author gives us a deeper understanding of the manner in which societies evolve institutions to enable them to deal with the basic problems of living and surviving. Such comprehension is essential to overcome prejudice and attitudes of condescension.

I am glad that in spite of the administrative burdens which Dr Parmar has shouldered as Chief Minister of his State, he has found time to continue his academic pursuits and make this valuable contribution to scholarship.

New Delhi

(Indira Gandhi)

INTRODUCTION

Polyandry in the Himalayas is an unusual book by an unusual author. In 1944 Yashwant Singh Parmar wrote a dissertation on "The Social and Economic Background of Himalayan Polyandry" which was accepted for the Ph.D. degree of the University of Lucknow. Thirty years later Dr Parmar has written this remarkable book, which uses his earlier study as the baseline for describing the institutions and customs of Himachal Pradesh with focus on the currents and directions of change in the last three decades. Between the first study and the present one Dr Parmar has remained in close and continuous touch with the people whose social profiles are presented in this book, but during this long association he has functioned not as an anthropologist or as a sociologist, he has been the principal actor on the political stage of the region and has contributed significantly to the shaping of Himachal Pradesh as we know it today. As Chief Minister of the state he has initiated and implemented policies that have brought economic prosperity to the people and transformations in their society. Preoccupation with the affairs of the state has not isolated Dr Parmar from the simple people of the hills over whose destinies he presides and whose social forms he has described in this book with great understanding and meticulous care in rich and vivid ethnographic detail. Not many administrators and politicians know their people as intimately as Dr Parmar does and very few among them have demonstrated the capacity to write on them with as much insight as he has done. Though claimed by politics, Dr Parmar has not been lost to Indian sociology; through politics and administration he has gained insights which are often denied to an academic researcher and these have enriched his analysis of the institutional base and social forms in Himachal Pradesh.

An admirable quality of this book is that Dr Parmar has

written with detachment and objectivity about sensitive social
practices such as polyandry, easy divorce and remarriage, and
allied customs which evoke understanding mirth and ridicule
in the people of the plains and whose existence is often denied
or apologetically and gingerly accepted as prevailing only in the
lower stratum of the society by the people of the region. He
does not shy away from the fact that such practices exist. He
not only describes them in all their regional variations but also
searches for the logic and the rationale behind their emergence
and persistence.

The society examined in this book is largely Hindu, but it
differs from the Hindu society of the plains in several aspects.
The castes are graded hierarchically into two main levels. Between the castes of the upper level there is considerable social
interaction and the barriers of endogamy are thin. For example,
the Bhat (enjoying a status analogous to that of the Brahman)
and the Kanet (claiming parity with the Rajput) can intermarry. Considerations of pollution and purity govern the two
main levels rather than individual castes on each of these
levels. Polyandry is practised by the upper level as well as by
the lower; all castes have the practice of *reet* in which a husband
can renounce his claim to the wife on payment of a customarily
determined compensation. All the groups feel the scarcity
and recognize the utility of women and broadly have common
norms defining their roles and obligations. A small but not
insignificant part of the population is Buddhist, but the social
forms and practices of the latter are in many ways indistinguish-
able from those of their Hindu neighbours.

Among the groups described by Dr Parmar fraternal polyandry is widely practised. The custom has its sanction in
mythology and legend. Draupadi, even though she was shared
by the five Pandava brothers, is even today the embodiment of
virtue and chastity for the Hindu women. The people of the
region continue to follow the example of these legendary
heroes. Until they were exposed to the outside world they felt
neither inferiority nor shame about this custom. With widen-
ing social contacts some people now have become self-cons-
cious about it, but most people in the interior continue to look

upon it with esteem rather than abhorrence. Of course, the important factors explaining polyandry in the region are biological and economic. In the parts where polyandry is in vogue, there is a definite demographic imbalance with an unequal ratio between men and women. The proportion of males is significantly larger than that of the females in several pockets and this necessitates the sharing of women by the brothers in polyandrous unions. Among the Buddhist groups several boys in the family take to a life of permanent celibacy by entering monasteries as Lamas, but even this does not solve the problem of unequal number of men and women and they also have to take recourse to polyandry. In the hills agricultural land is scarce and its cultivation is exceedingly difficult. Polyandrous domestic groups are more adapted to successful farming in the rocky slopes and narrow valleys. By pooling their labour and capital several brothers can attend to cultivation much better; single individuals may find the task unmanageable. The prevailing social practice definitely discourages fragmentation of land.

Polyandry cannot be understood without an adequate comprehension of the custom of reet. Reet permits a woman to secure release from one set of husbands to marry another. This custom ensures that each set of brothers would get, for some time at least, a common wife although there is no guarantee that she would stay with them permanently. Thus, reet extends the extent of sharing of scarce women by larger groups: polyandry enjoins that brothers have a common wife or common wives if they can afford them; reet permits the movements of women from one set of brothers to another in the course of her several marital unions after customary divorce. In a society which regards women as chattel—a commodity to be bought and sold—the practice of reet permits her release from inhospitable domestic environments and serves to demonstrate her value. There is, of course, the possibility of the custom being abused and of families disposing of women for temporary economic gain even though the women themselves may not desire such a move. Women are so highly prized that reet unions do not in any manner cause any stigma to them; they in fact put their price up.

I regard this book as a major contribution towards under-standing of a rare form of marriage and family in India. Dr Parmar has offered many perceptive comments on marriage in the region and has explained the patterns of adjustment within a polyandrous household with commendable precision and clarity. The value of this analysis is enhanced by the compara-tive perspectives that the author has presented on the forms of polyandry practised in small pockets in other parts of India. His exposition of the custom of reet, especially of its linkage with polyandry, its degeneration consequent on exposure to the outside world and to the acceptance of new economic norms, and of its implications for the status of women is extremely pro-vocative. I know of no other work which has probed this theme in such depth. The chapters dealing with changes in marriage law and custom and with modernization and social change are of special interest. Altogether the book provides valuable information on the life-ways in a remote and relatively in-accessible part of India.

Polyandry in the Himalayas is an important book and it will be read with admiration and respect.

Indian Institute of Advanced Study   S.C. DUBE
Rashtrapati Nivas, Simla 171005 (H.P.)

PREFACE

Polyandry is one of the rare forms of human marriage, and its practice has always attracted the attention of sociologists who have proposed many theories regarding its origin and continuity.

I have described polyandry as it was practised in the Western Himalayas in the late thirties when this work was first undertaken, and was later submitted as a Ph.D. thesis at the Lucknow University. However, this book is not the presentation of thesis in its original form since many changes—political, economic, and social—have taken place in this region after independence and the creation of Himachal Pradesh as a state of the Indian Union. All these changes have been incorporated in the present study and the whole perspective of the region has been brought up to date.

The book has been organized into two broad perspectives. First, it deals with the traditional social structure of the region as it existed during pre-independence days and, secondly, it discusses the major changes that have taken place during the last two decades which have transformed the region's political, economic, and social scene.

For a proper understanding of the changing society the ethnographic content of the book retains the social perspective of the late thirties. However, this itself has been described in the light of the changing geographical organization of the region. This adjustment in the description of the ethnographic material will enable the reader to grasp the past situation in terms of the present reality. In fact, the book presents a diachronic study of the Western Himalayan society where the traditional institutions, values, and beliefs are changing fast.

Y.S. Parmar

CONTENTS

CHAPTER ONE

GEOGRAPHICAL BACKGROUND

Along the northern border of India and within the mountain ranges of the western Himalaya is situated the state of Himachal Pradesh which was formed after independence by joining a number of princely states, namely, Chamba, Mandi, Suket, Sirmur, Bashahr, and 20 other smaller states in the hills as well as the hill areas of Punjab like Kangra, Lahaul and Spiti, and Simla. The state of Himachal Pradesh is rugged and mountainous. The northern border of Himachal Pradesh is bounded by Tibet, in the north-west it has a common border with Kashmir, and in the south lie the plains of Punjab. The eastern border of the state is common with the hills of Uttar Pradesh.

The state of Himachal Pradesh consists of ten districts with an area of 56,019 sq. km. and a population of 28,42,497. The district-wise area and population are as follows:

District	Area (sq. km.)	Population	Density per km.
Mahasu	5,844	3,58,969	61.43
Kinnaur	6,680	40,980	6.14
Mandi	4,196	3,84,259	91.60
Chamba	6,893	2,19,158	31.79
Sirmur	2,957	1,97,551	66.80
Bilaspur	1,163	1,58,806	136.55
Simla	1,281	1,85,194	144.57
Kullu	9,705	1,52,925	15.76
Kangra	7,715	11,24,202	145.71
Lahaul and Spiti	9,585	20,453	2.13
Himachal Pradesh	56,019	28,42,497	50.7

The people of Himachal Pradesh chiefly consist of hill Rajputs including Thakurs, Rathis, Rawats, Kanets, Ghirths, Brahmans, and Kolis or Dagis who are the menials of the hills. They are, either by origin or by long isolation from their neighbours of the plains, quite distinct from the latter in many respects and they speak Himali or Pahari of the western Himalaya speech within the Indo-Aryan family except in the northern parts where Tibet-Burman speech is spoken. They are almost exclusively Hindus but curiously strict as regards some ordinances of their religion and lax as regards others. The people are almost wholly agricultural though they supplement the yield of their fields by herding numerous flocks of sheep and goats by rude home manufactures with which they occupy themselves during the long winter evenings. They keep very much to themselves, migration being almost confined to the neighbouring mountains and low hills.

The hill Rajputs with their subordinate grades, the Rana, Main Rathi, Kanet, and Thakur are probably those who have retained their independence longest. A still older element in its population represented by Kolis, Gaddis, Girths, and Bahtis forms the bulk of its agricultural classes. The Brahman is found distributed all through over the states, viz. Kangra, Kullu, Chamba, and Simla districts where he represents a well-defined cultivating caste, distinct both from his namesakes who exercise sacredotal functions and from the secular castes. He is not, however, by any means rigidly endogamous and the Hindu population of this tract is singularly homogenous owing to the fact that hypergamy is the normal rule among all the castes.

The Khatri is indeed found among the Gaddis of Kangra but he is, if tradition is to be credited, a refugee from the plains whence he fled to escape Mohammedan persecution. The type of society found in the hills, no doubt, bears many resemblances to that feudal Rajput system which was evolved, as far as can be seen at present, after the downfall of the Kshatriya domination in the plains but it differs from it in several respects. In this tract we do not find a distinct Rajput caste which disdains marriage with the cultivating classes, but a Rajput class itself divided into two or three quite distinct grades.

The district of Sirmur lies in the midst of the outer Himalayan ranges between 77°5′ and 77°55′E and 30°20′ and 31°5′ N. Its length, as the crow flies from Kawal in the west to Barouna in the east, is 43 miles and its width from Damandar in the north to Baral in the south is 60 miles. The Simla hill states of Balsan and Jubbal form its boundaries on the north while the Tons river divides it from the Dehra Dun district on the east. The Jumna also forms its boundary line to the south-east.

The whole territory of the district is, with the exception of the Kiarda Dun, mountainous. It main stream, the Giri, enters the district at its northern-most point. It first runs from north-west to south-east and forms the boundary between Sirmur and Keonthal. Turning sharply to south-east it runs through Sirmur district and divides it into two almost equal halves—the Giri-war or cis-Giri territory, south-west of the river, and the Giri-par or trans-Giri tract, north-west of it. The residents of these two tracts differ considerably in their habits, manners, and customs.

The trans-Giri tract comprises the mountainous country with deep valleys lying between ranges of varying elevation which lie between the great range culminating in the Chur peak and the Giri river. From this great peak, 11,982 feet in height, run four lofty ranges. The first runs north-west, the Dhar Japroi Jadol, with its westerly spurs, the Dhar Pain Kuffar and Dhar Deothi. The second range, called Dhar Nohra, runs south-east to Haripur Fort (8,802 feet) where it divides into two ranges, one of which runs east to the valley of the Tons. These ranges divide Sirmur from the Jubbal. The third range, called Duddam Dhar, runs north-west and the fourth south-east toward the Giri. From Haripur Fort the Dhar Nigali runs southwards and then turns to the east under the name of Dhar Kamrau. North of and parallel to this range runs the Dhar Shillai and between these spurs lies the valley of the Niveli river which falls into the Tons.

By far the greater portion of the district is drained by the Giri or its tributaries. None of these is as important as the Giri except the Jalal on its right bank which joins it at Dadahu below Satibagh at the south-eastern extremity of the Sain Dhar.

On its left bank the principal streams are the Loja and Palor, which rise on the southern slopes of the Chur peak. The Giri is of varying width, in places 260 feet broad when in flood, but except in the rainy season it is for the most part shallow and easily fordable. During the rains its floods do great damage to the fields and houses along its banks. It is useless for irrigation until it reaches the Kiarda Dun. Timber in considerable quantities is however floated down it into the Jumna. Its water is supposed to cause indigestion, and has an unpleasant odour. It falls into the Jumna below Mokhampur. The Jalal, which rises below Nahi in Tehsil Pachhad, is a shallow stream of transparent water, rarely impassable even when in flood. Below Nahi, in the west, rises the Kawal, a stream which first flows westwards and thence turns north till it falls into the Giri.

The Tons forms the eastern boundary from Koti on the Jubbal border southward for some 30 miles, dividing the district from Jaunsar-Bawar. To the east of the Dhar Nigali rise two streams which flow into the Tons. These are the Bangal which drains the north-eastern corner of Jubbal, and the Niveli already mentioned. In the south-west corner besides the Markanda three seasonal torrents rise in the hills near Madhan Kidar and combine midway between Papri and Bhojpur to form the Run which flows southwards from the Dharthi Dhar into the Ambala district.

The above brief survey gives a general idea of the physical characteristics of the region which concerns us most. It is covered with a continuous range of mountains rising from the Giri river and culminating in the Chur peak, 11,982 feet high. On that lofty height can be seen from a distance the temple of Siva, Shrigul, which attracts pilgrims during summer when the magnificent scenery stands unrivalled. From the Chur peak can be seen the beautiful Himalayan hills lying around it as also the town of Simla, Sabathu, Solan, Dagshai, Kasauli, Kalka, Ambala, Sharanpur, Dehra Dun, and Mussoorie.

The whole area is occupied by a chain of mountains rising and falling in the midst of deep valleys and groves. The small hill streams worry the uninitiated visitor if he is travelling on foot. They make such a roaring noise in their downward rush over rocks and stones that one thinks one is to encounter mighty rivers but the water ordinarily never rises above the knees in the summer though in the rainy season even the smaller streams sometimes become unfordable because of their swift current. So the Giri, which is the largest of the running streams, causes in every rainy season a good deal of loss of human life and property. The higher hills are bare except for thin grass and a few trees but at certain places the grass is so thick that it is difficult even to pass over it. The forest near the Renka lake, the solitary but sacred lake in Sirmur (where a big fair is held every year in memory of Renka Ji, the mother of Paras Ram), abounds in wild animals of different kinds such as Bengal tigers, leopards, black bears, wild boars, swamp deer, barking deer, and jungle fowl. In the higher hills the hill goat or ghural, musk deer, black bear, and wild birds like Munal (also called Ratnal), Koklas, and Cher pheasant are common. The rivers contain many kinds of fish; the most important being Mahaser, Guja (eel), Sayol, Launchi, and Gunch. The flora is as varied as the fauna. Trees and plants of tropical regions are represented here. In fact, the altitude determines the kind of vegetation in different levels of the region.

The climate varies according to elevation. The tahsil of Nahan is fairly good but that of the Dun during the rainy season and the autumn is bad and malarial fever is prevalent. Tahsils Pachhad and Renka and the upper part of the Paonta are healthy. While the summer in the Dun is exceedingly hot, it is very pleasant in the hilly tracts. Pajhota, Sain, and the trans-Giri country are cool even in the summer. Trans-Giri records snowfall every year. The snowfall on the Chur peak is heavy from January to March and at times in April too. The zamindars dread the fall of snow in December but after December it is looked upon as beneficial, and the cultivators say it is as good as manure.

The main occupation of the people is agriculture. It is only in Nahan tahsil in which is situated the capital of the district that we meet any urban population. There is no other town and so practically every one in the tahsils has to depend on agriculture. The country being mostly rocky and mountainous, cultivation is very difficult. A spacious level field is rare. Ghanas (stone embankments) are constructed to make a field of about 20 to 25 yards. At places, to have more land for cultivation, people have constructed embankments as high as 40 feet to have just a small field. The agriculturist has to do all this because he does not have enough land for him. That is why villages are scattered and very thinly populated.

It is not the men alone who have to work hard in the fields; even the animals have to undergo immense strain in ploughing rough, sloping, and small plots. The peasants and their women have to put in additional labour in weeding out the stones from the soil. Ploughing is very difficult but it cannot be dispensed with. The hoe is, however, widely used. The agriculturist has thus to work hard for a hand-to-mouth existence. It may be noted here that the cattle of the hills, due probably to climatic and other regional factors and the hard labour they have to put in, are very small in size. They are kept in the ground floor of a residential house, or in a separate shed, called *obera*, which is made in or near the pasture. The cattle are usually left in those oberas or sheds without anyone to watch them. They are shut in so that bear or panther cannot do them any harm though at times due to some negligence a goat or a sheep is taken away at night. These sheds have small wooden doors and are warm even in cold weather. Well-to-do and industrious people keep buffaloes but not in the house. They are kept at a place not very far from the house where fodder is available in good quantity. This place is called *dochie* or *dera*. Here one member of the family takes the buffaloes or other cattle and looks after them. The goats and sheep are also taken there. The person in charge carries with him the wool that has been sheared from the sheep and while his cattle keep grazing he spins the wool on his *takli*. He thus utilizes his time and the wool when spun goes to make the warm coat called the *loiya* and the *dhabli* as also *cambul* and *pattoo*, i.e. blankets.

The people are thus poor and backward. One of the main causes of their backwardness is the absence of contact with the civilized world. There are hardly any means of conveyance and undeveloped communications have preserved the isolation of the hamlets which in turn have perpetuated ignorance and conservatism. The only means of transport so far had been the mule or pony. But it is not every one who can afford to possess them. Only the very well-to-do or the village *sahukars* (money-lenders) possess mules. Most people carry on their own backs their grain and other produce to the market. However, now the communication facilities have improved a lot.

A few Kanets and Bhats know Sirmuri, some of them know Urdu or Hindi, but few people get newspapers to keep themselves in touch with the civilized world. According to the figures for 1936-37, there was only one High School for the whole state at Nahan with 401 boys on the rolls. This school was run by the District Board. There are also three middle schools which are unrecognized, and one girls' school, and four unaided schools. Excluding the High School this gives a total of eight institutions with 317 students on the rolls. The total number of boys in all recognized, unrecognized, aided and unaided schools was 718. Out of a population of 148,568 only 718 students get the benefit of school education. The High School and the only girls' school are situated at Nahan proper, and the three middle schools are situated at Paonta and Sarahan which are not easily accessible to the students of the trans-Giri territory. For all practical purposes the trans-Giri people are denied all facilities for education. They had only two or three private and unrecognized primary schools aided by the District Board on account of the zeal of a few influential persons.

These schools did not generally engage the services of more than one teacher who was invariably not even a matriculate. With such educational facilities it is no wonder the people have remained backward and uneducated so long. The interest in education exhibited by some people appears, however, to be a happy augury and it seems that some progress towards education may be possible even without good communications. But, as it is, the people are very poor and backward. They have been, both mentally and physically, cut off from the civilized world. The comforts and luxuries of the modern world are quite unknown to them. They are simple, happy, and conservative. They have very few necessities. A loin cloth is usually sufficient to

clothe them, though they cannot do without a warm coat manu-
factured in their own homes out of the wool of their sheep. At
times it is the only clothing they have on them during the night
when the snow falls. It is used both in winter and summer. It
is the only woollen clothing they need and practically no cotton
clothes are used in the interior though near the Giri hand-spun
cotton clothes satisfy their needs. The women put on a sort of
skirt called *angulta*, a *ghagtu* under it up to the knees, and a
head dress called *dhatoo*. The ghagtu is now making way for the
pyjama. The people have simple habits and customs and pass
their lives quietly and contentedly. They live a communal life
on the Hindu joint family system without its modern drawbacks
and evils. The members of the fami y loyally, faithfully, and
cheerfully obey the eldest member of the family, called *Thagra*.

The religion of the people is mainly Hinduism and resembles
in many respects the Hinduism o f the Himalayas as found in
Kumaon to the east and Simla hills to the north, and is regarded as unorthodox by the Hindus of the plains. The Brahman
influence in this territory i s weak but the priests, Bhats, and
Kanets seem to wield considerable power over the people. They
have an effective caste hierarchy which for the sake of convenience might be divided into two main classes : the upper class
comprising Bhat, Deva, Dethi, and Kanet and the lower class
including Koli, Lohar, Badi or Bara and Bhadi, Bajgi, Daki or
Turi, Chanal and Dumra.

A word may also be said about the relations of the landlords
and tenants in the polyandrous tract of Sirmur in particular and
those of the other parts of state in general. The positions,
origins, and relations of Bhats, Kanets, Kolis, Dumras, and the
like in the caste ladder are discussed in the next chapter. It is
sufficient for our purpose in this chapter to note that the Bhats
and Kanets are found as landlords in the Himalayas and rarely
as tenants, while it has fallen to the lot of Kolis, Dumras,
Chanals, and the like to serve as tenants and have the Bhats or
Kanets as their overlords. The zamindards in the hilly tracts
settle Kolis and Chamars, as necessity arises, on their lands.
Tenants get food in t he morning and evening together with
clothes for the cold and hot season s and their dependents get

rent-free land according to their needs. They are advanced loans free of interest at their weddings and on other occasions though they have to render service in lieu of interest. Those tenants who serve the landlords after receiving a certain sum of money agree to place one or more members of the family, as occasion arises, at the service of the landlord and his or their services are credited as interest. If the tenants want to leave the land they have to pay back the money or go on serving the landlord till the doomsday. Such tenants are called Halis and the system is called Halip. A system very much like this was prevalent in Bihar among the Kamiyas. Halis have thus to keep serving their master or seek another on the same terms. Unless the debt is cleared they cannot leave his land. The system smacks of slavery and perpetuates economic servitude. It had been the practice in the past to pay the debts of the tenant before another landlord gave him protection and availed of his services. But the knowledge of their position and their legal rights has, to some extent, changed the situation. The tenants are now asserting their rights and leaving their masters. The landlords having lost their solidarity cannot now maintain their old position. In the past the state used to force the tenants to go back to the landlord unless his debts had been paid but now the landlord is instructed to approach the law courts. He cannot have any real help from the law courts for the tenants possess nothing but their own persons and thus no decree of a court of law can help the creditor. Since the landlords, in the higher polyandrous regions in particular, depend for cultivation mainly on Halis this has greatly affected their position.

In some cases it is indeed a great hardship on the zamindars. Some of them invest all their life's savings in Halis and if a Hali runs away there is no means of recovering the amount advanced to him. Cases have been known where zamindars have advanced as much as Rs 1000 to a Hali. On the other hand the case of the Halis is also a sad one. They become hereditary serfs to all intents and purposes. Moreover, the helplessness to which they are reduced by the burden of a debt they can never repay deserves the sympathies of all.

Besides the Hali there is the Dahialta. He is in a much better position. He tills the land and pays to the landlord according to the terms of his agreement a half or two-thirds of the produce at each harvest. Otherwise he is quite free to do as he likes, though on occasions he too works for his landlord. Unlike the Hali, he owns some property. The zamindars advance loans to Dahialtas to settle on their lands for purposes of cultivation. They gradually pay back the money but as a rule stick to the land they settle on. Their problem is not so serious as that of Halis. But of late, owing to scarcity of labour, zamindars are at places finding it very difficult to keep all their cultivable land under the plough without their help. A zamindar cannot till all his lands himself and so he has to engage Dahialtas for the purpose. But the most unfortunate part of the situation is that they are getting scarce. There are many reasons for this maladjustment of labour in this state but the important one is that in certain parts malaria and venereal diseases are gradually reducing the population and people from other parts of the state do not like to come and settle in such unhealthy places. The consequence is that while there is a surplus of labour in certain portions of the district, Tehsil Nahan and Pachhad suffer from shortage of it.

Nevertheless, this system is an improvement on the Halis for the Dahialtas have opportunities to clear there debts and be masters of themselves. Besides these, there is the blacksmith, carpenter, barber, shoemaker, potter, and blanket-maker who settle in the villages as menials. The blacksmith or *bandhi* gets 16 seers of grain for each plough, the shoemaker 16 seers for each man and eight seers for each woman, and the barber five seers per head. The village artisan works in the same old style and has not improved his art with the times. He gets his wages according to the practice of the region. He is paid for his services in kind, not in cash, at harvest time, i.e., twice a year. He has thus no incentive to increase his skill or efficiency under this system. But now he prefers to work on contract basis or daily wages. Since, as a rule, the professional work does not yield him enough for his living he takes to cultivation also. He does not take much interest in his profession and hardly ever fulfils his engagements within the given time. This naturally upsets the employer and he engages some other worker. He is thus deprived of his professional work. Each village menial also gets a rupee or 50 paise at the wedding of a boy or a girl respectively. In the case of hired labour the rates of wages in kind vary with the status of the land-owner and the nature of the work. *Kamins*, i.e. menials, are feasted on the first day of every month and on holy days. Daily labourers are not employed for agricultural work. Kolis generally work for the landlords in return for a share of the produce, and they are indispensable for every village. Extra labourers are required to help in ploughing, manuring, and weeding and for this neighbours are invited. Someone plays the Dhol or Nagara and the rest work, all receiving some *sattu* (roasted powdered grain) at noon and a meal in the evening. This system of securing the help of neighbours in their agriculture and other works, such as the construction of a house or conveyance of timber, is called Hela. It is a system based on a communal tie and is very economical. In a country where hired labour is not available and the means of the people are limited it would be impossible to venture on any work of importance that requires men and money. But these people have devised such a simple but effective cooperative method that no difficulty arises in their day-to-day working. Whenever any work of importance is to be carried out the neighbours are invited to do it. They are given sattu in the morning and their meals in the evening and after a well earned smoke they return home. This sort of arrangement is a common and usual occurrence and has kept the village community intact.

CHAPTER TWO

POLYANDROUS CASTES—A BRIEF ETHNOGRAPHIC SURVEY

BHATS

The Brahmanic influence in this cultural region, as has already been mentioned, is weak though the caste hierarchy exists and has not been effectively wiped out through disintegration. The two most important classes, the upper and the lower, consisting of Bhat, Deva, Dethi, and Kanet on the one hand and the Koli, Lohar, Bhadi, Bajgi, Chanal, Dhaki, or Turi and Dumra on the other, form the bulk of the population. Even in the most backward tracts where the influence of the Brahmans is weakest and where the whole system of living is influenced by communal ties, we find evidence of caste rigidity. None but the Bhats, Devas, and Kanets can enter a temple. The Kolis or any other low caste cannot drink at the same source with Bhats and Kanets. In order to understand the position of each caste or tribe in the social ladder we have to study their customs, manners, and origins separately.

The one fact that strikes a visitor in the polyandrous tract of Sirmur in particular and the Simla hill tracts in general is that hardly anyone calls himself a Brahman or Rajput. The use of the word "Brahman" is confined mostly to those who live in the towns or villages inhabited mostly by immigrants from the plains. In the rest of the country they are known as Bhats. The same is the case with the Rajputs. It is only those who belong to the ruling house who generally call themselves Rajputs, the others being ordinarily called Kanets. The two terms have for practical purposes become synonymous though a certain stigma attaches to the Kanets. The Kanets, Rathis,

Rawats, Negis, and Thakurs hold a somewhat similar status and the names are in most cases used as synonyms. We shall, however, deal with them while discussing Kanets, their origins, status and position in the caste hierarchy. We have mentioned above that all the Brahmans formerly called themselves Bhats and so we had very few Brahmans entered as such in 1901. There were in all 2,669 Brahmans in Sirmur in 1901, 2,398 in 1911, and 2,562 in 1921. But with a growing feeling that they were as good as Brahmans and there was, in fact, no distinction between them some of them refused to be classed as Bhats and had themselves entered as Brahmans in the census of 1931. The result was that there was an immense increase in their numbers and from 2,562 in 1921 they rose up to 10,987 in 1931. While the number of Bhats which was 16,513 in 1901, 18,090 in 1911, and 17,652 in 1921 fell to 9,532 in 1931. But since the authorities would not enter the Kanets as Rajputs the census figures did not show much difference in their numbers.

It has been admitted on all hands that the Bhats are by origin Brahmans and no one has yet suggested that they are not Brahmans. They enjoy the same status and position here which their counterparts do in the plains. They stand highest in the caste ladder and no auspicious function can be performed without them. In Chamba, as in Sirmur, the Brahmans form an agricultural class though they form the apex of the caste hierarchy. Those who live in the capital are employed in the services or engaged in trade, while others are very poor and eke out a living as priests in the temples, or as *purohits* or even cooks, but they abstain from all manual labour. In Sirmur, however, they perform even manual labour. Strict in caste observances, they accept the ancient Brahmanical gotras but are divided into various *als* which form three groups. The first two have no caste relations with the third. The Brahmans of Chamba town and Sungal eschew all caste connections with the *hal-bahu* or cultivating Brahmans who can hardly be distinguished from the general rural population though many of them act as priests at the village shrines and as purohits. In Sirmur, however, the hal-bahu are not looked down upon simply because of their profession and have connection with the town Brahmans. The hill Brahmans, both men and women, eat meat in marked contrast to those of the plains. It is only the Pabuchas of Sirmur, with whom we shall deal later, who among the hill Brahmans do not eat meat. In the polyandrous trans-Giri tract of Sirmur inter-marriages between the upper classes, i.e. Bhats and Kanets, are common and no caste rules forbid them.

It has been said that the Bhats of Sirmur are by origin Brahmans but, having adopted *karewa* or widow marriage, they have lost their status and are by occupation genealogists. It has, however, to be borne in mind that they have lost their position only in the eyes of the Brahmans of the plains for among the hillmen the Bhats hold exactly the same status as the orthodox Brahmans do in the plains. A stranger may at once notice their superiority in the caste ladder. It is a common spectacle in the hills that the mightiest and most respected of the Rajput or Kanet over-lords wish *palagan*, i.e. *paon lagan* (I touch your feet) to any Bhat who happens to come across him. No respect is considered greater than touching the feet. It is only the parents who receive that honour. The average hillman does not confine himself to merely folding his hands and bowing when he accosts a Bhat but addresses him with palagan and the Bhat, though just a youngster, gives his *ashirvad* or blessings to the man. It is the Bhats who always have precedence at all social and other functions none of which are complete without them. Though poverty and ignorance have adversely affected them materially and spiritually they have retained their high position and command the greatest respect and esteem in society. They assign a reason for their being called Bhats. In the hills a Bhat is one who can cure people of the influence of *pariyan* (evil spirits) and practises the Tantric Vidya or black magic, *jantras* and *mantras*. Originally the Kolis and Dhakis used to engage in this business and were called Bhats. The Rajputs, Kanets, and Brahmans also learnt it from them. The Brahmans, being the most intelligent and educated community, specialized in the profession and practically ousted the Kolis and Dhakis from it. The result was that the Brahmans came to be called Bhats and in course of time acquired this name for their profession. The explanation is supported by the fact that even now we find that some of the Kanets, Kolis, Dhakis and even Chamars, who follow this profession, are called Bhats. We came across a case where a Bhat Brahman, who wanted to utilize the services of a Koli to work as a Bhat and help him to get rid of the influence of evil spirits, approached the district authorities to permit the Koli to visit his village and treat him. The application was granted and the Koli Bhat went to the village and did his job. The Bhats who work as priests in temples are known as Devas. They have formed a class of their own though they intermarry with Bhats. A Kanet cannot serve as a priest in a temple although investigation revealed some laxity in this respect. In Mail Kanets can become Devas. In Charna Bhawae also Kanets become priests of Shrigul. At Jamun, Renka Ji, and Manal too Kanets become priests. The Kanet who serves as a priest is called a Negi who should always marry a Negi girl though this rule is no longer observed. The Dethis stand lowest among the Brahmans. They were originally *Charjas* or persons who performed the religious ceremonies of the dead only. They are, however, treated as equal to the Bhats though they are considered the lowest. The Deva stands between the Bhat and the Dethi.

One important and influential, though numerically not very strong class of Bhats, is the Pabucha. Pabuchas are considered a little higher than the ordinary Bhats. They are more orthodox in their religious and social observances and so enjoy a superior position. They take their meals in their Chauka and do not take meat like Bhats. They trace the origin to *Parthiv*, i.e. worshippers of Shiva-lingam. They do not intermarry with Bhats. It was however found that Pabuchas gave their daughters to Bhats as also took theirs in marriage. But a Bhat girl who marries a Pabucha will not take meat at her husband's home though she may take it at her parents'. Similarly, a Pabucha girl who marries a Bhat will not take meat when she is with her parents but she may when she is with her husband. The Pabuchas do not intermarry with Kanets. The other Bhats,

except those who are near the cis-Giri, do. In Sirmur Bhats
intermarry with Kanets freely only in the trans-Giri territory
but they smoke together and take both kachhi and pakki
roti cooked by Kanets in other parts too. They drink water
brought by a Koli in a metal vessel and prepare their food
in the house of a Lohar, Bajgi or Koli when it has been
plastered with cow-dung.

According to the *Sirmur State Gazetteer*, if a person marries
one of a lower caste he is expelled from his caste, but if
he merely cohabits with one of lower caste, he is excused.
When an accusation of this kind is brought against a person,
a panchayat is convened to hold an enquiry. If the allegation
is proved the accused is made an outcaste, but if it is disproved,
the complainant is made to pay a fine. Not only does that
man become an outcaste but all those who eat, drink or smoke
with him are also considered outcastes. If an outcaste desires
to re-enter his caste he again convenes the panchayat and
craves forgiveness. If his fault was unintentional, he is made
to give a dinner to the *baradari* and to feast Brahmans. Sometimes he is also asked to bathe in the Ganges. But if the
offence was intentional, he must perform a *praschit* (penance),
bathe in the Ganga and give a feast to Brahmans and the
baradari. In either case a he-goat is sacrificed. In trans-Giri
this latter panchayat should consist of the members of at least
four Khels. In Nahan and cis-Giri more orthodox measures
are taken to readmit an outcast. There excommunications are
strictly enforced and serve to maintain the caste barriers.
There is, however, one exception to the general rule, that
one should not marry a person lower than him in the caste
ladder. In the trans-Giri tract a Bhat can marry a Kanet
girl and vice versa, but the *Sirmur State Gazetteer* says that a
Kanet by marrying a Koli becomes a Koli, a Bhat becomes
a Kanet by marrying a Kanet, and so on. In the trans-Giri,
especially in the interior, the Bhat and Kanet are considered
equal as far as marital ties are concerned and a Bhat marrying
a Kanet does not become a Kanet. There the determining factor
is the caste of the husband. If a Bhat marries a Kanet girl he
remains a Bhat but the woman takes the caste of the husband

and becomes a Bhat. So too a Bhat girl by marrying a Kanet husband becomes a Kanet and is thus absorbed by the caste of her husband. She may also leave her Kanet husband and then either remarry a Kanet or a Bhat.

A concrete example may illustrate how the custom acts in practice. One Tulsi Ram, Brahman (Bhat), resident of Paloo, Tehsil Pachhad, a place in the trans-Giri tract of Sirmur, had married Diwari, sister of Mani Ram, Brahman (Bhat), resident of Kothia Jajar in the same tract. As Tulsi and his wife Diwari could not pull on well, Diwari left him and went back to her brother's place. According to the custom, when they had agreed to part, a bargain was struck and Tulsi renounced his rights over her and agreed to receive Rs 260 as Reet for his wife. One Ram Sukh, a Kanet by caste, resident of Barbia in the same tract sought her hand, made a bargain with Diwari's brother, paid him Rs 260, and thus became her husband. The former husband executed a deed in his favour renouncing all his rights over Diwari. A day was fixed on which Ram Sukh was to go to her place and bring her to his house. On the appointed day he reached there but the woman was missing and it was found that she had eloped with another youngman, Bhoopa, a Kanet by caste, resident of Kothia Jhajar, the same village to which Diwari belonged. This Bhoopa, though a Kanet, was a brother-in-law (wife's brother) of Mohi Ram, Brahman (Bhat), an uncle of Diwari. Mani Ram and Mohi Ram, brother and uncle of the woman, realized another sum of Rs 260 from Bhoopa and let him have Diwari as his bride. Ram Sukh, the unfortunate sufferer, lost his bride and his money. He sought the aid of the criminal courts from where he could get little redress. The interesting part in this particular case is the free relationship of the Bhats and the Kanets. Mani Ram, Mohi Ram, and Diwari are Bhats. Diwari who first married a Bhat remarried a Kanet and refused to be his wife on the ground that he was her maternal uncle. She bestowed favours on Bhoopa, whose own sister had married Mohi Ram, uncle of Diwari. Thus, a Bhat girl may marry a Kanet and a Bhat may marry a Kanet woman as Mohi Ram had done without in any way running the risk of losing her or his caste. But

the same would not be the case if a Bhat woman or man
married a Koli husband or wife. In that case she or he would
be at once excommunicated. One Mata Ram Bhat had a Bhat
wife named Munni. For some years they lived together as
husband and wife and had children. In course of time they
had differences and their relations became very strained. A
Koli, Matoo, one of their tenants, utilized this rift between
them to win her favour and, though much younger to Munni,
made advances to and developed intimacy with her. She fell a
victim to this young man and, having cast her traditions and
principles, openly violated them and started living with him.
The husband and the community, enraged by this outrage,
held a panchayat and excommunicated her. Not satisfied with
this, the husband lodged a complaint against the seducer under
section 498 I.P.C. and had him convicted. The woman is
now living with her son. She is called Kolan Bhatni and
has become the object of great ridicule. Similar would be
the case if a Bhat married a Koli girl or a Kolan as she is
called. But if he merely develops intimacy with her and has
even sexual relations with her he is not excommunicated,
provided he does not go and live with her or eat and smoke
with her. A carnal relation alone would not make him liable
to excommunication but eating and smoking with her would
certainly make him lose his caste.

Sexual relations with the lowest of the order (i.e. Chamars)
are not tolerated and if a Bhat or even a Kanet develops
intimacy with a Chamar he or she is liable to be excommunicated. Intimacy with a Turi woman is not considered objectionable
provided one does not eat or smoke with her. A man's intimacy
with a woman of lower caste, provided of course he does
not eat or smoke with her, is considered much less objectionable than a high-caste woman's intimacy with a man of lower
caste. The moment this intimacy is accompanied with eating,
drinking or smoking together the person makes himself or
herself liable to excommunication. Free relations exist between
the Rajputs and Brahmans in some parts of Chamba state.
In the Pangi tehsil of Chamba district Brahmans, Rajputs,
Thakurs, and Rathis form one caste, without restriction of

food or marriage. In the Ravi valley especially in Churah, and to a less degree in Brahmaur also, free marriage relations exist among the high castes, good families. But in recent years there has been a tendency towards greater restrictions on the observance of the caste rules.

In addition to providing brides to Bhats and Kanets Bhat girls were also given to the members of the then ruling family and their children were called Kanwars. The girls were given with the bride as *khawas* or *dasi* (slave girls). Kanet girls also were taken as khawas in this manner as well as by payment of Reet. Their children, designated as Sarteras, could not inherit property. They were merely given maintenance at the sweet will of the father. Though they were styled Kanwars and received some consideration they were an unfortunate class which had sprung up as a result of this practice. They did not have the slightest right to the property of their fathers who at times are found to hold them dearer than their lawful sons. This subject will be more fully dealt with in a subsequent chapter.

In the upper hills of Bashahr it is common for Brahmans and Rajputs to marry Kanet girls. Such marriages are in a sense regular, but the children of the union are designated Sarteras. It is not, however, uncommon for the descendants of a Sartera to gain the status of his father after three or four generations. There are concrete instances of this in the case of some of the ruling families in the hills. A raja or a rana was succeeded by a Sartera son and the latter's descendants had in course of time been accepted in marriage by Rajput families.

In Kulu the children of a Brahman and a Rajput by a Kanet woman are called Brahmans and Rajputs respectively and the term *Rathi* is often added as a qualification by anyone pretending to unmixed blood. In the absence of other children they are their father's full heirs but in the presence of other children by a Lari wife they would ordinarily get an allotment by way of their maintenance.

Bhats of the trans-Giri tract of Sirmur, unlike the cis-Giri Bhats, practise polyandry as the other Kanet and Koli castes do and have adopted the customs and manners of the Kanets.

How polyandry affects their household management and working will be considered in another chapter.

KANETS

Kanets are the yeomen of the state. On the west they extend as far as Baghal and the eastern portions of the Kangra valley occupying the whole of Kullu, Mandi, Suket, the Simla hills, and Sirmur. They form more than half of the population of the Simla hills and Sirmur. A few are also found east of the Sutlej in the Jhandbari and Kotaha valley. In Kangra proper their place is filled by Ghirths. Rajputs are, generally speaking, their over-lords but in many places, especially in the Simla hills, they have retained their original independence. According to a popular version on which much stress has been laid by the *Gazetteers of the Simla Hills,* the original inhabitants of these hills were the Khash, a people without caste or class distinctions. Whether they were or not of Aryan stock is not stated but they were presumably of the same race as the Khasias of Kumaon and Garhwal who are generally supposed to be Aryans. The Khash began by being self-governed by the panchayat system but gradually leaders sprang up in the persons of Mavis or Mavanas some of whom are supposed to have been Jat immigrants from the plains and other masterful individuals of the Khash tribe itself. The Mavis formed small confederacies and lived by preying on one another. Eventually they were overthrown by Brahmans and Kshatriyas whom the pressure of Muslim conquest drove up from various parts of India.

Among the most notable differences from Brahmanical ordinances (which they had developed) are the practice of polyandry, the neglect to wear the *janeo* or a sacred thread, the liberty given to a wife to leave her husband and marry another man if the latter compensated him for the expenses of his marriage, and the dropping of orthodox funeral ceremonies. Many of these are Aryan customs long since abandoned in the plains. Sexual lapses were not taken so very seriously in early Aryan society and a certain amount of promiscuity prevailed. In the *Mahabharata* (Book I, Chapter 122) it is stated that women in primitive times were free and not bound to be faithful to their husbands. They could have intercourse with any man they chose, even though they were bound by ties of marriage. This custom was abolished by Svetaketu, son of Uddalaka who probably voiced public opinion that had been formed on the subject but had remained inarticulate. This shows that the primitive Aryan society probably passed through a stage in which promiscuity was tolerated as a necessary evil, if not approved.

The same account states that the term *Kunit* was first applied to Brahmans and Rajputs who, in a strange country peopled by a primitive race, abandoned the orthodox tenets of Hinduism and lapsed into such practices as widow remarriage. Many explanations of the word are given. One is that Kunit means violator, i.e. of the Shastras. The Rajputs or Chatris who did not observe the Shastras strictly are said to have been called Kunit or Kanet. Their laxity was mainly with regard to wedding and funeral rites and in taking widows as wives. Another explanation is that the word is really *kania-het* (love of daughters) because Kanets did not kill their daughters. The true Rajputs used to kill theirs at birth. A third suggestion is that "ait" signifies sons, just as "aik" signifies brothers and kinsmen, e.g., Ramait means Rama's sons and Ramaik his brothers and kin. Now Raja Kans of Puranas is called Kan in Pahari and his sons would be called Kanait, but since Kans persecuted Brahmans and was looked upon as a *dait* (devil) he was killed and left no descendants. Others say that Krishana, also called Kan in Pahari, invaded Bashahr and advanced to Shurintpur (now Sarahan), so his descendants are called Kanaits. But neither suggestion appears tenable. Sir Denzil Ibbetson is of the opinion that something like what happened to the Gorkhas of Nepal has happened with the Kanets. He says that Rajputs merely consist of the royal families and that a tribe of any caste whatever which had in ancient times possessed supreme power throughout any fairly extensive tract of country would be classed as Rajput. Some of the so-called Rajput royal families were, according to him, aboriginal, notably the Chandel.

According to Alexander Cunningham the Kanets were the

descendants of Kunindas or Kulindas, a rich and powerful people who ruled about B.C. 1500 between the Bias and Tons rivers,
and that they were the original inhabitants of the lower slopes
of the Himalayas from the backs of the Indus to the Brahma-
putra. Their country was called Kauninda with its headquarters
at Sugh near Buriya in Jagadhari tehsil, Ambala district. A
number of coins of the king of Kunindas were also found by
Cunningham near Buriya.

It is also suggested that the word "Kanet" is derived from
kanishta (junior cadet). Sir George Grierson however points out
that the derivation, though phonetically possible, is improbable.
From Kanishta one would ordinarily expect some such word as
Kanet has a dental Tunaspirated. There are, he says, isolated
instances of such changes, but they are rare. In the countryside we were told that the explanation of the word Kanet is
to be found in the use of the bow called *kan* by these men and
that since the hill Rajputs were all excellent bowmen and still
use the bow at festivals and rejoicings, they were called *kanait*
(bowmen). Grierson also mentions a class of messengers in
Bihar called Kanait (bowmen) from *kan* (arrow) and perhaps
Kanet may have a similar origin.

While Cunningham has fixed the date of the kingdom of
Kunindas approximately at B.C. 1500 it appears that this community called Kulindas held very great influence earlier in history. Cunningham thought that Srughna was the capital of their
kingdom but it might in fact have been no more than the headquarters of one of their districts for their kingdom lay stretched
in the Himalayas between the Meru mountain to the east of the
source of the Ganges and Mandar, a little to the west of the
source of the Bias river. Map No. 2 in *Historical Atlas of India*
(S.J. Charles Joppen, 1915) illustrating ancient Aryan India
shows the area held by the Kulindas at that time and it coin-
cides with the area in which the so-called Kanets are found to
this day. In his note on ancient Aryan India in the same Atlas
Joppen writes: "The Kashmira occupied the upper valleys of
the Vitasta, Asikni, and Urungira, the Kulinda the mountains
west of the Ganga sources." Their position and social status can
further be determined by a few slokas which we find in the

Mahabharata (*Sabha Parvas,* Chapter 78, T.R. Krishnacharya and T.R. Vyasacharya). When Duryodhana addresses his father at Raj Suya Yagna he says:

> *Merumandaryo madhye*
> *shailodamabhito nadim*
> *Ye te kichakavenunam*
> *Chhayam ramym upaste* (78)
> *Khasha ekasanadyarha:*
> *Pradara dirghavenava:*
> *Paradashcha Kulindashcha*
> *Tankana: Partankana:* (79)

(Between the Meru and Mandar mountains and on both sides of the banks of the streams with cold chilly waters of the hills in the beautiful shade of the bamboos are such Khash, Kulinda, Parada and Tankana castes as are equal to us in status and suppress the enemies.)

The use of the word *ekasanadyarha* by Duryodhan is significant. Ekasanadyarha literally means one who is eligible to sit on the same seat and, since only those holding equal rank and status can sit on the same seat, it shows that the castes of which he speaks are equal to him in position and status. When we bear in mind that Duryodhan was proud of his rank and position and would not easily recognize any caste or tribe as being equal to his own we realize the position and status of the Kulindas at that time whom the proud king admits as equal to the royal family of Hastinapur. No better status could have been possible than that of the ruling family of Hastinapur to which Duryodhan and the Pandvas belonged and the Kulindas must be presumed to have held the same position as the Kurus and Pandavas on the testimony of Duryodhan himself. We come across slokas to the same effect in the *Mahabharata* (Sabha Parva, Chapter 29, Slokas 27-44). They also speak of the Kulindas as rulers of the land. It can thus be assumed that the Kulindas were an influential Aryan people at the time of the *Mahabharata* who held rank and status equal to the Kurus and

Pandavas and ruled a kingdom in the Himalayas where we find the Kanets at the present day.

Some of the Simla hill states in their Gazetteers mentioned that there are no Rajputs there, but Kanets only, except the members of the ruling family. The distribution of Rajputs and allied castes shows a curiously small number of Rajputs in the hills states. There only the ruling families are Rajputs, the mass of the peasantry being Kanets or Ghirathis, if indeed these last can be separated at all from Rathis and Rawats. Ibbetson identified Rathis, Rawats, and Thakars, which is another name for Kanets, with Rajputs. With Rajputs he took the Thakar, Rathi, and Rawat who are lower grades of Rajputs rather than separate castes. The line between Thakar and Rathi may be roughly said to consist in the fact that Rathis do and Thakars do not ordinarily practise widow marriage; though the term *Rathi* is commonly applied by Rajputs of the ruling houses to all below them. Again the line between the Rathi and Kanet is exceedingly difficult to draw, in fact, in Chamba Rathi and Kanet are considered identical and are said to inter-dine and intermarry, and it is said that Rathi is, in Chamba and Jammu, only another name of the same people who are called Kanet in Kullu and Kangra. Thus no Kanets but numerous Rathis are returned from Chamba. On the other hand, none of the other hill states return either Thakars or Rathis, having probably included the former with Rajputs and latter with Kanets.

KOLIS OR DAGIS, DHAKIS AND TURIS

Bhats, Brahmans, Kanets, and Rajputs form the upper group while Kolis or Dagis, Dhakis and Turis, Dumras, Badhis, Chanals and Chamars form the lower group of people. Kolis are numerically as also from considerations of agriculture the most important of the lower group. As will be found from the following pages it is not very easy to determine their definite status in the caste ladder. The term *Koli* is used in three distinct senses. First, as a territorial term it denotes a resident of Kullu. Lyall speaks of the Rajas of Kullu as Koli Rajas. He adds that the name Koli is applied outside Kullu to any Kullu-man, but Kola would appear to be the more correct form. A Kullu-man has also been called Kulluta. Lyall was of the opinion that Kolis were not of pure Rajput blood and were probably Kanets by origin. It is said that they were for some time petty Thakurs or barons of the upper Kullu valley. Secondly, the term denotes the Koli of the hills who is practically the same as the Dagi or as the Sippi in Chamba. Thirdly, it is used for Chamars in some parts of Punjab who have taken to weaving.

It is possible that the Kolis of the hills are identical with those of the plains or both are so named because they follow the same calling. Ordinarily, however, the designation Koli is supposed to have been derived from "Kulin" degraded from a family, i.e. a Malecha or Sudra. They are probably so called because they work as menials and are looked down upon by the higher classes. The Dagi is an off-shoot of Kolis and derive the name most probably from *dangar* or *daga* (cattle). Dagis dragged away dead cattle and were thus called Dagi. A Koli who took to removing dead cattle would be called a Dagi. One account connects them definitely with Kanets. It is said that once a great cattle disease affected the countryside. Cattle died in every village in great numbers. Chamars could not cope with the situation and remove all the carcases. A very awkward situation was created. No one could take food till the carcases had been removed from the house. The people took counsel and devised means to get out of the difficulty. Some Kanets offered to remove the carcases from the houses. They removed them but they became polluted by touching dead cattle. They were shunned by the other Kanets and were termed Kolis. They are thus degraded Kanets but retain their gotras which are the same as those of Kanets. Some Kolis have also Shandilya and Kashyap gotras. Another very common story prevalent in the Simla hills and Sirmur about the origin of Kolis is that a Kanet father had two sons by two wives. He divided his property between them. It was decided that whoever ploughed the field first in the morning would get the first share. The younger brother got up early in the morning and ploughed the field. When the elder brother woke up he found that the younger one had already got up and was busy with his plough. In order to steal an advantage over him he started ploughing the courtyard. He, however, found the courtyard too narrow and in a fit of anger killed the bullock with an axe. He was turned out of the caste for this. He had two sons, one living a respectable life, while the other was guilty of skinning and eating dead oxen. From the first son descended the Kolis. They do not generally perform any menial work and Kanets will drink but not intermarry with them. From the second son descended Dagis who skin and eat dead cattle. They are further sub-divided into Dagoli and Thakur. The former do not eat with the latter because they eat and drink with Mohammedans.

From the above account it would appear that it is not quite easy to trace their origin definitely but it seems clear that they have a good deal of Rajput and Kanet blood in them.

Careful enquiries were made about Kolis but except some knowledge of the working of this caste, their manners and habits, hardly anything has been added to what has already been known about them. Apart from the different stories current about their origin it appears that due to their contact with Kanets and Bhats some Kanet and Bhat blood may be running in their veins. Whether they belong to the great community of Kols who lived in India or to Kolis or Koris is still a matter of conjecture. It is, however, clear that this community is a mixture of many castes and tribes and has absorbed all sorts of people in its fold. The Bhats and Kanets who lost caste easily found a place in this order. Their women were attractive enough and were in some cases successful in winning the attention of a Kanet or Bhat with the result that he was excommunicated and ultimately received by Kolis in their order. Their physique, colour, and features, while indicating a good deal of mixture, suggest some affinity to Kanets and Bhats.

While in Kullu, Saraj, and other areas Koli and Dagi are used as synonyms, in Sirmur Koli and Dhaki are used in practically the same manner. Even the Turi, a separate class, have not been considered as different and have been enumerated with the Koli in the last census. Koli, Dagi, Dhaki, Turi, and Chanal are not synonyms though they are practically used as such to describe the lower classes of menials of the higher hills. The Koli is generally considered to be the highest of these though at some places even that is doubtful. For our purposes Koli, Dhaki, Turi, and Chanal are all important as in the trans-Giri these castes practise polyandry and some of their practices are noteworthy in that connection. They are, however, so intermixed that it will be best to deal with them together.

The trans-Giri Kolis perform marriage according to the Jhajra and follow it up by Reet. The cis-Giri Kolis, however, perform a virgin's marriage always according to Phera and only the next marriage, whether as a divorced wife or as a widow, is performed according to Reet. The Kolis of Nahan consider themselves superior to those of cis-Giri and trans-Giri. The Kolis of cis-Giri in their turn consider themselves superior to those of cis-Giri and trans-Giri. The Kolis of cis-Giri in their turn consider themselves superior to trans-Giri Kolis and do not ordinarily intermarry.

Cis-Giri Kanets and Bhats do not ordinarily drink water brought by a Koli but they, like Rajputs, do not object if it is brought in a metal vessel. This restriction is, however, disappearing even in cis-Giri. While the high castes do not eat food touched by Kolis they may prepare it in a Koli's house when it has been plastered with cow-dung. A Koli must not let his shadow fall upon any person of high caste. Nor can he and the other menials, except only Turis, use gold ornaments. At weddings Kolis, unlike their overlords, have to go on foot or on ponies. They can neither use a *palkee* (palanquin) nor play a *naquara* (kettle-drum). The Kolis of Nahan proper claim the use of palanquin and naquara but the mass of Kanet and Bhat population, as also Rajputs, do not concede to them this right. In the countryside a Koli could use a palanquin or a naquara only when he had obtained permission from Kanets and Bhats, had arranged to carry the Kanet or Bhat, his overlord, in a palanquin leading the *barat* as a mark of honour and respect to the community. and had also paid some offering. If this was not done the palanquin could not be used nor could the naquara be played.

The mass of Kanets and Bhats are sentimental and sensitive on this point and an attempt by the Kolis of Nahan to break this practice resulted in a clash of these communities. Attempts were made by the more broad-minded of them to let Kolis have these rights but nothing came out of them.

Kolis serve their Kanet, Bhat, and Rajput overlords as Halis or Dhialtas. When there is a marriage in the family of their overlords they have to carry palanquin, beat the kettle-drum, and play the Narsingha. The Koli is thus a constant companion to Kanets and Bhats and he is very helpful to them in their day-to-day life. Even at the time of death he has to collect wood for the funeral pyre. He is thus indispensable to the landlords, especially of the hill tracts, and it would be difficult for the latter to carry on agricultural operations without him. His relations with the landlords are not so strained as they would appear to be at first sight. There certainly are social barriers which divide them but on the whole in their daily life these hardly seem to take away their good feelings and understanding of each other. Though Kanets and Bhats take work from them it is not true that they are cruel to them. They mix with them freely and though they do not smoke with them in the same *hukka*, the *chilm* in which the tobacco is smoked is passed on to them too. They help Kolis at the time of their marriages and deaths and meet all their needs. If a landlord cannot help his Koli at the time of need he gets a bad name in the *ilaqa*. Some Kolis are very well disposed and would stick to their masters through thick and thin. It is only in towns that one notices any estrangement of relations. In the ilaqa one rather notices a cordiality which could hardly be expected.

It has been noted by Sir Denzil Ibbetson that in Sirmur the Koli occupies a position below the Lohar, Badi, and Bajgi but above the Chanal and Dumra. The Badi or Bharai is hardly a distinct caste in this area. It is a division based on a professional basis. Any one who takes to wood-cutting or carpentry is a Barhai. Mostly Kolis take to it. In Kullu they have no scruples about eating the flesh of dead animals but such is not the case in Sirmur.

The *Bajgi* (musician), i.e. the Turi, stands in a different position but can hardly be said to be superior to a Koli. From a study of the working of these castes, it can hardly be said that the Koli stands lower than the Lohar, Badhi, and Bajgi in Sirmur. On the contrary, he would seem to stand at the top of the lower classes. The case of the Bajgi or Turi is of course slightly different as will be noted later.

The *Sirmur State Gazetteer* has not treated Turis, Dhakis, or Bajgis as a separate caste and has considered them with Kolis. They are a class of village artisans and, though a small community, have their own importance. Their main function, as the name Bajgi, i.e. musician, indicates is to play music. They are not an agricultural class like the Koli but live by musical performances. It is the Turi who plays the flute and naquara at weddings and also beats the drum when a corpse is carried to the burning ground. Turis get a share of the offerings to the dead and receive the shroud besides fees in proportion to the means of the deceased. As they take the offerings to the dead they are considered unclean and rank a little lower than the Lohar in the hills. They also generally do sewing work and are the tailors of the hills. They marry in their own community and in the upper hills a Kanet may not even cohabit with a Turi woman although in the lower hills he is not excommunicated for doing so. Their women are also proficient in music and give performances. A Turi girl is the only low-caste woman who is allowed the use of gold ornaments. Turis are very good as musicians, especially at the tabla, naquara, and the flute. A few of them have created local reputations for themselves.

In Punjab Lohar is a separate class but not so in the hills. The Lohar of the Kullu hills is probably a Dagi who has taken to the blacksmith's trade and so lost status for Dagis of the present day will not eat with him. Lohars do not even eat the flesh of animals who have died a natural death. In Lahul Lohars are not numerous and they rank below Dagis. A Dagi will however marry a Lohar girl but not vice versa and a Dagi and Lohar will smoke together from the same pipe. In Spiti the Lohar, Zon or Zobo, stands midway between the Chhazang and the Hensi or Betu. A Chhazang will eat from his hands but intermarriage is deprecated.

Lohars are skilful smiths. They make pipes, timber boxes, buts, locks and keys, knives, choppers, hoes, ploughshares, chains, scythes, axes, and swords. Some of their handiworks are of quaint and intricate patterns. They get wages for their work in the shape of grain. When they work at the employer's house they also get food. At harvest time they receive a share of the produce. They marry within their own tribe or with Badhis or Barharas, i.e. goldsmiths. Kanets and Bhats and other higher castes do not eat or smoke with them. They cannot wear gold ornaments. They are a small community.

In the higher Simla hills Lohars intermarry with Barhis, i.e. masons, and a Barhi can enter a kitchen of higher caste person with his tools in his hands to effect repairs but a Lohar cannot do so. Barhis my wear gold ornaments but may only don a *sehra* (chaplet) of flowers by permission and Lohars are equally subject to this rule. Neither caste marries with Dagis or Kolis.

DUMRA OR DUM OR DOM

The Dumra, Dom or Dum of the hills is considered one of the lowest in the caste hierarchy. He forms a link between the Koli and the Chamar. He is a *Chuhra* (scavenger) of the hills though he has hardly to do the work of removing night-soil. He is found in the higher hills of Chamba as also in the sub-montane tracts of Kangra. Like the Chuhra of the plains he is something more than a scavenger. Whereas the Chuhra works chiefly in grass, the Dumra adds to this occupation the trade of working in bamboo. He makes sieves, winnowing pans, fans, grass-rope, strings, matting, baskets, screens, furniture, and other articles which are made of bamboo. In the lower hills he is called Bhanjra where he confines himself to this kind of work. In Sirmur he is mainly an agriculturist and works on the fields of his Bhat or Kanet landlord. He has to perform all kinds of menial work for them. He is an untouchable and Bhats and Kanets do not eat or drink at his hands. He cannot go with shoes on in the presence of Bhats and Kanets and has to take off his shoes and move aside in making way for them. Like Kolis and other low castes he has to offer the ordinary salutation of Samaniya and has to be barefooted at that time. A Dumra woman cannot wear gold ornaments. Dumras are not allowed to live with Bhats or Kanets and have to live apart from the rest.

Dumras are said to be the descendants of the aboriginal race which enjoyed at one time some power and importance. They are regarded now as unclean. While the Koli appears to have a good deal of Aryan blood in him the Dumra is an aborigine, pure and simple, and does not seem to have any Aryan blood in him. He is generally very dark, with irregular features and thick hair. A Dumra girl too is very dark though she has fairly good features. A Dumra is considered to be very witty, clever and good at repartee. Dumras marry within their own groups and cannot intermarry with Kolis. Even Kolis do not eat at their hands nor would they smoke with them. This community too is polyandrous.

CHANAL

Between the Dumra and the Chamar, the lowest caste, is found the Chanal. It is a small community found both in the hills and the plains. The term *Chanal* has been derived from the Sanskrit word *Chandal*, which means a person whose occupation is carrying out corpses and executing criminals and other abject offices for the public service. It is the menial class of Kangra and Mandi. It corresponds to the Dagi in Kullu and the Koli in the Simla hills. But in Kangra as also in the Simla hills and Sirmur he is inferior to the Koli. Some of them however do not touch dead cattle nor mix on equal terms with those who do. The Chanal of Mandi will not intermarry with a Dagi of Kullu. On the whole he stands lower to the Koli, especially in Sirmur.

CHAMARS

The Chamar, as in the plains, is the tanner and leather worker
of the hills. He is untouchable and stands lowest in the caste
ladder. The name is derived from the Sanskrit *Charām-kara*
or worker in hides. In Sirmur he holds the field as a tanner and
a leather worker but since this does not give him enough
for his living he takes to agriculture also. In the plains he
is most useful as an agricultural labourer. In the hills however
his services are needed most in his orginal profession and
since he has to satisfy the needs of the whole village community
he is very much in demand. Every village has not a Chamar
while there is no village where cattle do not die. As no
other community would remove dead cattle from the shed,
not to speak of skinning them, the person concerned has
to wait till his Chamar from some other village comes and
does the needful. He has to supply shoes to his employers
who give him grain at harvest time. He also receives some
grain on all festivals and marriages.

Since the Chamar stands lowest in the caste ladder he
has to build his house away from the village at a spot where
only persons of his community live. A separate place from
where he can draw water is allotted to him and no other
caste would even touch that water. He is generally dark in
colour and is almost certainly of aboriginal origin, though
in his community may be found members of high castes who
have fallen or have been degraded. Intermarriage with higher
castes is absolutely forbidden and even sexual intercourse is
not tolerated. Anyone who breaks the rule meets with
immediate excommunication. Even a little laxity in this matter
is not allowed and anyone who continues the relation is sure to
lose his own caste and sink to that of the Chamar's. Like
the Dumara the Chamar women cannot use gold ornaments. A
Chamar cannot come with shoes on in the presence of a Bhat or
a Kanet and has to offer the usual salutation barefooted. Like
the other communities Chamars practise polyandry in polyandrous tracts but not in the cis-Giri tract.

CHAPTER THREE

ECONOMIC IMPORTANCE OF WOMEN

The position of a woman in society has been variously estimated and diametrically opposite views are current regarding her place in different stages of civilization. On the one hand, she is conceived as little better than a slave or beast of burden, condemned to perform the hardest drudgery, bought as chattel, and treated as such. On the other, those who have had anything to do with tribes reckoning descent from the mother are likely to view a woman as the undisputed mistress of the family, if not of the communal life as well. Both concepts are, as far as the vast majority of the people are concerned, bound to be far away from the actual state of affairs. There is so much variability in the relation of woman to society that any general statement must be taken with caution. Her utility, her resourcefulness in domestic life, her refreshing company and the affectionate care of children have always proved to be a great asset to her partner in life and have, to a considerable extent, determined her status at different stages of civilization.

In the hill society of the region a woman appears to be subservient to man, is regarded as chattel and bought and sold to the highest bidder, and may be inherited by her husband's kin. If the husband wills it, he may repudiate his marital obligations and divorce her on the flimsiest pretext, and receive compensation for her in the shape of Reet. True, a woman in these areas can be sold to the highest bidder like chattel if the husband wants it but he can hardly afford to do so. She is so much in demand because of her social and economic utility that a husband cannot do without her and cannot dispense with her services. On the other hand, she agrees to stay only as long as she finds things agreeable and the slightest provocation may induce her to leave him, go to her parents,

arrange to pay Reet to her husband, and find a new husband
more to her liking. The same is the case when she is an inheritance of the kinsmen of her husband on his death. She is inherited by them only when she wants to live with them; she is
at liberty to find someone who would be prepared to pay Reet
for her. Reet for a widow is less than that for a woman having a
husband alive. It is her choice that matters and if she does not
want to live with her husband or her husband's kin nothing can
force her to do so. The husband or his kin in Sirmur can refuse
to accept a certain amount of Reet as being inadequate for her
release and she cannot remarry and be free till she has obtained
a release. She can however behave in such a manner that her
husband or his kin would in most cases be forced to give her a
release. The husband needs a wife mainly to look after his
household and to perform domestic duties, as also to bring in
fuel and grass, graze cattle, and help him in the various agricultural operations. The sexual need does not play a very important part. The woman, after obtaining a release, leaves his
house and goes to stay with her parents. The injured husband
could have redress from her if she remarried. But she would not
remarry though she may develop intimacy with someone secretly or even openly. Her relations and neighbours would not go
against her and even if the husband were to take the matter to
a law court he would be disappointed for lack of legal proof of
adultery. As a result she would continue to live with her parents
without any formal divorce or remarriage and the husband
would be deprived of her services for which he primarily needed her. He would under such circumstances take the matter
more philosophically, and agree to accept Reet for her and give
her the liberty to remarry. With the money thus obtained he
may get another wife and thus set his house in order. The
woman is in fact mistress of the situation and uses it to her own
advantage. She is on the whole an equal partner with her husband and does not suffer from any serious restrictions or handi-
caps. She goes with her husband to the fairs and festivals and
to the bazaar for shopping. There are no restrictions to her
appearing in public. She entertains guests and attends to their
comforts. In short, she is free to do all sorts of work and her

drudgery is in part compensated by her independence and freedom. This status may to a considerable extent be due to her economic utility to her husband who has to depend on her. We must, therefore, study the employment of women in the hills to get at the root of her status in society. In order to illustrate her importance in the society we have to consider the question from two standpoints: her utility in the domestic circle and her contributions to field and other outdoor operations.

The bearing of children and their upbringing, and the affectionate care the woman takes of them is the same everywhere. But her daily routine from morning to night in the hill society has a specific character. In the morning her first duty is to attend to the cattle. She milks the cows and buffaloes and cleans the *obera* (cattle-shed). The refuse of the cattle is taken out and dumped at a place from where it is later conveyed to the fields to be used as manure. She feeds the cattle and generally looks after them. After milking them she takes them out of the obera and the young boys or girls are deputed to look after them. She then attends to the kitchen and there the milk that had been coagulated in the night is made into *cha* (butter-milk). Butter is separated from the milk and the butter-milk is used for drinking. The butter is turned into ghee for consumption by the family. Sometimes the butter is sold in the market or to the village shopkeeper or sahukar. Having finished this she goes out with her scythe to the fields to cut grass for the cattle. The calves and disabled cattle are not taken out and they have to be fed indoors. She has also to bring water in earthen pitchers from the spring near the village. She next engages herself in the kitchen and prepares the morning meal. The food is very simple consisting mainly of maize-bread, rice, *dal* (pulses), and vegetable. The morning meal consists of sattu or in winter at times of boiled *gaugti* (Arum Colo-casea). That does not take her very long to prepare except on festive occasions when she has to cook the whole day to entertain guests. She is now free to go out and proceeds to bring in fuel and grass. In the evening she has to milk the cattle again. The cows and buffaloes are generally milked three times a day—morning, noon, and evening. After preparing the meal for the night she keeps hot water ready for

the bath. The men, tired after the day's toil, come at nightfall
and to relieve them she provides them with a hot bath. Those
who do not take a bath simply wash their faces while she
washes their feet. She keeps the milk for coagulation before
retiring to bed and this finishes her daily routine. She has very
often to do some other work which is quite as important. She
has occasionally to rinse the house with cow-dung solution
while the kitchen has to be cleaned every morning. The produce
brought from the fields needs drying up to protect it from an
early decomposition. She, therefore, spreads it on the roof of
the house or in the yard specially made for this purpose. The
rice brought from the fields has to be threshed and winnowed.
It is her duty to do it. In the social sphere, in so far as it affects domestic work, her duties are hardly less useful. At the time
of marriage or at festivals when guests have to be entertained
she bears the brunt of the burden. If guests are few she attends
to them all by herself and prepares for them dainty dishes like
the *askalyan*, *patanda*, *dharoti*, and the like. Askalyan is a standard dish for festive occasions. It is made of ground rice and
the food is peculiar to the area. Cup-shaped depressions are
made in a round piece of stone called *askali*. Small earthen cups
are made to cover the depressions. The askali is put on the
hearth till it becomes hot. The powdered rice is mixed with
water and the solution is put into the depressions in the askali
and covered with the earthen cups. Salt or sugar and dry fruits
are mixed in the solution to make the food tasteful. When the
covering cup is turned red by the heat of the fire in the hearth
it is placed on the askali and is removed only when the solution is found cooked into a hard stuff called the askalyan. If
sweet or saltish it is taken with ghee or *dahee* (curd) but if not
it is taken with *urd* (phaseolus radiatus) preparation which is
made specially for it. An askali has at most ten or 12 depressions and it takes a pretty long time for it to get heated enough
to cook the askalyan. Women have to spend a whole night for
the purpose in order to feed the members of the family and the
guests next morning. The same amount of labour is required for
the preparation of patanda, another hill speciality. To make it,
ghee is applied to a hot iron pan and *atta* (wheat flour) mixed

in water is carefully spread with the fingers on the entire pan. The process needs great skill. The merit of the preparation lies in producing very thin patandas. The solution has to be evenly applied on the hot iron pan with the tips of one's fingers. A little carelessness may result in the fingers getting burnt. A slight even pressure of the fingers is used for spreading the mixture on the pan. When baked, the patanda is ready for use. It is prepared only on festive occasions by women; men rarely prepare it. The guests are served mainly with such delicacies as are prepared laboriously by women. The Toda women, while they are well treated, rank as inferior to men and are excluded from the ritualistic observances that occupy the foremost place in Toda culture. They are indeed left with very little employment on their hands, being debarred even from cooking, at any rate when the food contains milk as an ingredient. The women of the Himalayas are not bound down by any such restrictions and play their part in every household duty and activity.

They add not a little to the happiness of society by their participation in *gee* (local dance). Marriage festivities would not be complete if women did not have their dance called the *parooha*. Practically all the women of the village participate in it some way or other. They have also to perform the *sohag lagana* of the new bride which can be performed only by a married woman or a virgin.

It is not only as a worker at home that the services of the woman are demanded. She is as important in the fields as at home. Near the obera the refuse of the cattle is collected in a place called *gabraos*. She carries this on her head or at times on her back to the fields where it is utilized as manure. A woman in the cis-Giri is not expected to do this sort of work to allow which is considered unchivalrous on the part of men. But in the trans-Giri tract or Sirmur and in the other Simla hill states it is different. After the manure has been collected and the field has been ploughed by men she breaks the lumps of earth that are left behind by the plough. The stones in the field are thrown out by her to prepare the soil for the growth of the crop. When the plants grow four inches in height the *godai* takes place which is carried out by women by means of a hoe. Wild herbs and superfluous plants that grow with the crop are weeded out. This process is valuable from the point of view of cultivation, for on it depends the success of the crop. In rice cultivation also women are useful. When the fields are flooded and are ready for the rice plant women have to do the transplantation with the help of a basket called *poora* or *poori*. It is a very tedious, trying, and laborious process and needs careful and constant attention till the whole field is finished.

Apart from the usual management of the household a woman has to do other work from morning till evening. It is worth noting that women perform almost all tedious tasks because they need not much strength but careful attention. The women of Kanaur are, however, physically as strong as men and carry out, as we shall see later, work which needs great strength and endurance. When the crops ripen the services of women come in great demand and they come out in large numbers with their scythes to cut the crop. It is again a very important work for which they prove very useful. While men work in the fields, their women carry their meals and hukka from home. When the oxen thresh the corn a woman leads them round and round. After the crops have been cut and the corn threshed she has again to help her partner in carrying the produce home from the fields. Nor is this all. She has to perform in the Himalayas a task which is spared her elsewhere. She has to take the corn to the village mill and after it has been ground into flour to carry it back home. In those areas where wild animals destroy the harvest at night she keeps vigil to scare them away from the fields. With a torch made of *Bihul* (pine twigs) in one hand and a stick in the other she carries on this tiresome work the whole night and at times cannot afford to have even a wink of sleep lest wild animals damage the crop and the poor cultivator be deprived of his season's earnings.

Women are a source of help not only in the household and the fields but also in the industrial undertaking of their partners. They take an active share in the manufacture of mats and baskets. In Bashahr, Mandi, and other areas, where sheep-breeding is done on a large scale, they help not only in supplying fodder to the sheep and in looking after them but do a considerable part of the spinning and weaving as well. A weaver's wife is very helpful in his profession and he would find it hard to pull on with his work without her active help. In Bashahr, Chamba, and Mandi states women help their mates in wood-chopping. While men fell the trees they do the slicing, and help them in turning out timber using a big saw with which they cut wood with extraordinary ease. But what may seem surprising is that they carry such heavy loads as put men to shame. They carry the timber on their backs from the place where it is sawed to the place from where it is to be floated down the river. Kanauri women with heavy logs of timber on their backs are a familiar sight in the hills. One will find them cheerful and smiling and prone to exchange words even with strangers while carrying heavy loads on their backs. They have been seen carrying logs weighing anywhere between 200 to 300 pounds with perfect ease and equanimity.

Thus it is that the woman works. There is no restriction on her except one. She is nowhere allowed to plough the land. If under extraordinary circumstances she is obliged to do so, it is taken as an insult to men. This brief description of her work goes to show how, in the region, she is man's equal in every respect. She works everywhere, performs all kind of duties, and helps man in every possible manner. She is of immense utility to man and that is the reason why she is always so much in demand. One finds it extremely difficult to carry on one's agricultural operations or other undertakings without the help of one's mate. She participates in all social and religious functions. She attends the various festivals far and near with her partner. She takes part in singing and dancing. On festive occasions she joins the native dance called *Raga* or *Gee*. Whenever a sacrifice has to be made to some deity she accompanies her husband to the place of worship. Her activities are in no way limited and she shares equal opportunities with man. She does the shopping herself and sells or barters the produce of the fields. She naturally deserves some compensation for the hard work that is her lot and thus she enjoys a liberty which is denied to her in orthodox society. The free open-air life makes her very hardy and strong and fit for the work she has to perform. By her econo-

mic utility she is equal to man in every respect and treats him
just as her equal. Added to these the scarcity of her sex en-
hances the demand for her and her position in society is
assured.

Polyandry in the Himalayas, as elsewhere, has been attributed
to the poverty of the people. It has been practised long in some
areas of Himachal Pradesh and it is worthwhile noting its
effects on the life of the hill people in the various phases of
their activities. A glimpse at the economic effects may lead to
a better understanding of the people.

That the custom originated in the scarcity of land and of
women coupled with the extreme poverty of the people goes
without saying. It will also be seen that it is only because of
the prevalence of this custom that such a large population in the
remote mountains is supported. The sub-division and fragmentation of holdings was certainly avoided and a check placed on
the partitions of families as also of property. Those who would
not have been by themselves able to pay for a bride, without
whom they could not run the household or the farm, were enabled to have the services of a mate by clubbing their resources
together. Thus far the custom seems to have achieved its
object. But the scarcity of women kept a number of men still
without wives. Women, conscious of their utility to men and
the freedom natural to open-air life, developed an independence of outlook which was absent in orthodox Hindu society.
A woman would not stick to a husband or a number of husbands who did not agree with her nor would any man like to
keep a woman who would prove disagreeable to him. The
result would be that she would go to her parents and refuse to
live with her husband or husbands. It was mainly in expectation of her services in the house and in the field that she had
been married by her husband and he could not for long afford
to keep her idle at home. He would either persuade her to return or release her from his marital bond and receive compensation so that he could spend the money on getting another wife.
By this method a person would be enabled to get another wife
and one who would never have been able to get a wife would
also get a chance to have one. This system called Reet is not

attended by any formal ceremony and marriage is dissolved when a woman takes a new husband by paying the first husband the money originally paid to her parents and so long she is in demand this sum goes on increasing after every such marriage. In the beginning the custom did not present very many difficulties and worked smoothly along with polyandry. The sum of money paid as Reet was not high, rarely being above Rs 70. But gradually it increased to Rs 100 or Rs 200 and finally to Rs 1000 and even Rs 2000 during the late thirties, in the case of a specially prized beauty. Thus the working of this custom took a new and unexpected turn. The contact of the rich and unscrupulous people of the plains with the poor, starving people of hills had very disastrous effects on their lives. A woman was already in demand because of her scarcity and utility. The rich men from the plains found that they could get women for comparatively smaller sums and with greater facility in these areas than in the plains. They could always outbid the poor local peasants and offer better attractions to women in the shape of a higher standard of living. The amount of Reet was thus considerably enhanced and the monetary side of the transaction, which was so long confined to the expenses of marriage, assumed greater importance. The husband wanted money if he had to release his wife not only towards the expenses of his previous marriage but also to provide for another wife and pay his debts. By this process the monetary consideration became prominent and had dire consequences for the people. It has often been said that the custom of Reet has led to the indebtedness of the people and has ruined family solidarity. Very few people, however, care to understand how it really works and whether there is indeed any truth in the charge. Had a Reet marriage been confined to a woman only once or twice in her life it would not have led to any serious consequences. For an average peasant in the hills it is difficult enough to find money even for one marriage in his lifetime and that is why he has to pool his resources with others so that he may pay for a wife. But if he has to pay for a bride more than once he is doomed. The women of the hills do not, however, content themselves with marrying once or twice according to Reet but, as every subsequent Reet adds to her attraction, she must marry as many times as she can find new husbands willing to pay for her.

Massamat Shibi of Naini Dhar in trans-Giri tract of Sirmur had as many as 16 husbands in her lifetime. But leaving aside the question of the morality of such transactions we have to consider the effects they have on the economic life of the country. Take an example. B married a woman A. He spent Rs 200 on her marriage. After a year the woman leaves him and settles Reet with him. The bargain is struck at Rs 200, the money spent by him. But the poor man had borrowed that sum at an interest of 25 per cent per annum and had to pay Rs 50 as interest to his creditor. He thus remains indebted to the extent of Rs 50. C pays her Reet and takes A as his wife. He gives a feast to his friends and spends about Rs 100. For three years they pull on well but then fall out. A goes home and does not return. The divorce negotiations start and the Reet sum is fixed at Rs 250. D offers to pay this sum. C had borrowed Rs 200 for the Reet money and Rs 100 for the feast and has to pay Rs 225 only as interest at the usual rate of 25 per cent. He gets only Rs 250. We have also to consider the Reet tax, amounting to 15 per cent, which the husband has to pay every time as it was levied by the then Sirmur state government. Further, an ordinary villager is a notorious spendthrift and the moment he has money he squanders it. When he gets the Reet money he does not always pay his creditor but spends it and remains indebted all his life. Six families or more may in this manner be engulfed in debt simply because a particular woman does not stick anywhere and, because of her demand in society, had bidders always at hand. It is not a rare phenomenon but one which is found abundantly in the hills. One person near Bhavai in Renka, Sirmur, paid Rs 600 as Reet for his wife. He mortagaged his landed property, the few bighas he held. But before six months elapsed the woman went away and would not come to him. He had mortgaged his land in the hope of managing his household but lost both his wife and homestead. Much as he tried, the woman would not come while the interest on the money borrowed increased every day. He was without hope and left home to earn something by service to keep body and soul together. A woman in Thanga in Sirmur is said to have been instrumental in depositing Rs 500 in the shape of the Reet tax in the state treasury, and the most interesting feature of the case is that she married in the same village every time so that not a family was left in which she had not lived as a wife. Since Rs 500 went to the treasury at the rate of 15 per cent it is evident Rs 3,333 has in all been paid by the various husbands towards her Reet. In 1925 the income from the Reet tax in Sirmur was about Rs 32,000. In other words, the people of Sirmur spent Rs 213,333 towards Reet and got indebted practically to that extent. In 1926 they paid Rs 34,000 in the shape of this tax and the husbands in all spent Rs 226,666 as Reet. In 1938 the income from the Reet tax in Sirmur was Rs 22,000 which means that the people spent Rs 146,666 as Reet.

When we realize that most of this money is borrowed by a people who can never have the means of repaying it we are no longer puzzled to find them permanently in the grips of debt. Most of the tenants are, due to this chronic indebtedness, at the mercy of their landlords. They have to serve their masters in return for the money which they borrow to get wives. A tenant can have this loan either by serving as a Hali or as a Dhialta. As a Hali his wages cover the interest alone. There is no likelihood of the debt decreasing, but if he has to remarry, in case of his wife's death, or his son has to marry he may borrow afresh and the total sum will bind him and the generations to come for ever. He cannot leave his master without paying his debts. If he goes to another person's land he borrows from him the money he has to pay his previous master, agrees to serve the new master as a Hali, and thus gaining liberation from the one binds himself as a slave to the other. The condition of a Dhialta is much better for he gets the produce of the land and pays one half or one third of the produce to the landlord according to the custom. He has the possibility of saving a little and by hard labour and frugal living can repay his debts. He too borrows from the landlord and if he cannot pay him he cannot go anywhere else. If another landlord needs his services he will advance him the money to clear his debts. But while theoretically there is a difference between the two systems, they are very much the same in their working and have resulted in the enslavement of the tenantry. The result is that the mass of agriculturists are in debt and there is very little hope of their being ever freed from it. While considering the indebtedness of tenants we cannot afford to ignore some other factors which have contributed towards it. An agriculturist borrows because he has some needs to satisfy. He borrows for his current needs and he may borrow because he has credit and cannot resist the temptation of making use of it. He cannot keep any accounts, for he is illiterate, nor can he distinguish between productive and unproductive debts. He has to depend solely on nature and that again affects the character of his credit. The risk run the lender, the period for which a loan has to be granted and the absence of any organization which could participate actively in agricultural finance leave the field open to the moneylender and he exploits the position to his satisfaction. The moneylender wants his profits which are determined by the security which the borrower offers him and the amount of cash he has with him. The agriculturist needs money for domestic requirements also but he can pay his debts only at each harvest, i.e. twice a year. Apart from his domestic requirements he may be forced to borrow because of the vagaries of nature. The loss caused to him by the failure of one single crop is such that for years he is unable to make it up. The epidemics may ruin his family or destroy part of his capital such as cattle. He has to fight these calamities single-handed and whenever they make their appearance he has to seek the moneylender and borrow for his needs. If this debt is fairly large he is hardly able to pay it back in his lifetime and passes on the burden to his successors. Many an agriculturist thus starts his career with a heavey burden of ancestral debt.

CHAPTER FOUR

TYPES OF MARITAL RELATIONSHIP—
POLYGYNY, POLYANDRY, AND DIVORCE

Marriage is preceded by betrothal in every society though the customs and practices with regard to it differ. The parents regard it their duty to see their sons and daughters married and even if they are poor they would rather incur debts to do their duty than bear the opprobrium of society for shirking what as parents they are required to perform. The notion has a greater hold where the mass of population is uneducated and conservative. Whether a man can afford the expenses or not he must get his sons and daughters married so that he may not be looked down upon by society and fail in his duty to his own self. Thus many families incur debt and court poverty because of the marriage expenses but they cannot tolerate the idea of having an unmarried boy or girl in the family. They would prefer death to this humiliation. The same idea has penetrated into the trans-Giri society where people are found to carry it to excess.

While in the plains the age for betrothals and marriages is going up everywhere these people stick to their old practices and ideas. Betrothals take place very early. In some parts of the trans-Giri territory a betrothal is arranged before the child attains the age of one year. As soon as a child is born it is sometimes betrothed. Not only that, betrothals are known to take place even when the children are in their mothers' wombs. The understanding in such cases is that if the babies belong to opposite sexes they are to be wedded to each other. The actual ceremony is, however, performed after the birth of the babies. (The table overleaf elucidates the point.)

Even when the children were only one-year-old 44 of them had been married. Their betrothal must have taken place some-

Age	Population			Unmarried			Married			Widowed		
	Persons	Males	Females	Persons	Males	Females	Persons	Males	Females	Persons	Males	Females
Total	139,031	76,922	62,109	42,766	26,239	16,527	83,471	45,650	37,821	12,794	5,033	7,761
0-1	3,230	1,658	1,572	3,186	1,617	1,569	44	41	3	—	—	—
1-2	3,179	1,631	1,548	3,073	1,542	1,531	106	89	17	—	—	—
2-3	3,541	1,761	1,780	3,353	1,625	1,728	186	136	52	—	—	—
3-4	3,611	1,771	1,840	3,267	1,562	1,705	342	208	134	2	1	1
4-5	3,566	1,804	1,762	3,102	1,540	1,562	457	261	196	7	3	4
0-5												
Total	17,127	8,625	8,502	15,981	7,886	8,095	1,137	735	402	9	4	5
5-10	15,394	8,246	7,148	11,257	6,224	5,033	4,097	2,001	2,096	40	21	19

SOURCE : *Sirmur State Gazetteer*, Part B, 1931.

time before they were born. There were 106 married persons of the age of 1-2 and 188 of 2-3. The figure goes up in the case of persons of 3-4 years: they number 342 while persons of 4-5 years number 457. Thus between 0-5 years of age we find 1,137 married persons and most of these belong to the trans-Giri territory. Between the ages of 5-10 we find the figure rising to 4,097 out of which 2,001 were males and 2,096 females. It is thus clear how very early betrothals and marriages take place in this country. Children are married when they are yet in their cradles and it is interesting to find persons who are widowed before they leave their cradles. There were two widowed persons (one male and one female) between 3-4 years and seven (three males and four females) between 4-5 years. It would be sheer cruelty if in these circumstances no widow marriage were sanctioned by society and girls were forced to live as widows all their life. Naturally widow marriage in such society is a common and daily occurrence.

The betrothal ceremony is a simple affair. The bridegroom's people send their *Purohit* (family Brahmin) and barber with some ghee and a lump of sugar to the bride's place. If the bride's people after consultation accept these articles the proposal is complete. Some people send clothes, myrtle, *mauli* or *paranda* (red, yellow, and white threads stitched together) and even cash. The bridegroom's parents must present clothes to the bride at every Diwali after the betrothal ceremony till the actual marriage otherwise the betrothal will not stand. The boy is at times made to work with the parents of the girl when he is too poor to make any presents.

Betrothals are of two kinds: (*i*) *kachhi*, i.e. preliminary and (*ii*) *pakki*, i.e. final. All that is necessary for a preliminary betrothal is that a man is sent by the parents of the boy (if he has none living, he goes himself) to the girl's parents with some kachha ghee, a few rupees, and a *bheli* (a lump of coarse sugar). No particular relation or person need carry these things for the boy. If these are accepted, the matter ends there. At the time of final betrothal some money in cash, a bheli, a pair of silver bangles, a *hanɔli* (tight necklace), and three garments—*kurta* (loose shirt), pyjama, and *chaddar* (sheet) to cover the head—

are sent through a pandit and two men to the house of the betrothed girl. Paranda and *mehndi* (henna powder) are also taken. The girl's side is represented by a pandit and two of her relations. The pandit from the girl's side puts on her arms the pair of silver bangles (*kangan*) sent by the boy. A pujan is held. Swastibachan, Ganesha Puja, Khotshe Matrika, Kalash Nwagrah, etc., are also performed. After the betrothal till the marriage is celebrated the boy or his parents send one complete suit consisting of kurta, pyjama, and chhadar to the girl thrice a year at Diwali, Bishoo (1st of *Baisakh*), and Rihali [from *hariyali* (greenery), held on the 1st of Sawan every year]. If no separate pakki betrothal is held, the ceremony of giving the bangles, etc. is performed at the time of marriage. In cis-Giri the age at betrothal varies from five to 15, but Rajputs, Bhats, and Kanets celebrate betrothal and marriage between 15 and 20, both ceremonies being performed simultaneously. It is customary in trans-Giri to take bride-price, only Rajputs avoid the practice. Brahmans and Banias as well as Kolis and other artisans and trading castes practise it. This money is paid to the bride's father or the nearest male relative by the bridegroom. Pun marriage, in which the parents of the bride receive nothing in cash or kind from the bridegroom, is confined to the upper classes, but the rest consider themselves entitled to receive some compensation for the upbringing of their daughters. Even when anything is received as compensation, the amount is not very high and only marriage expenses are charged. The Bhats and Kanets usually avoid it but their indigence forces some of them to have recourse to this help. Insanity, leprosy, or any other incurable physical defect in the boy or the girl entitles either party to cancel betrothal. Otherwise it is regarded as an offence to cancel a betrothal without sufficient and cogent grounds. Great offence is done in wantonly cancelling a betrothal but the discovery of physical defect in the boy or the girl is held to justify it.

Betrothal followed by marriage at an age of one to ten years may seem to be a horrible practice and grave consequences may naturally be apprehended. But the custom does not materially affect the social life of the people for the girl is not allowed to cohabit with her husband before she attains puberty. Though women here are at the mercy of their husbands and can be deprived of the marital protection at any moment, they enjoy great personal liberty. Their status here is in certain respects superior to that of the women in the plains. The natural result of early betrothal and marriage would have been the permanent slavery of the girl-wife under her husband and members of his family and she would have found it impossible to extricate herself out of this intolerable life. But what actually happens is that when she attains majority or understands her own interests she can dissolve the marriage contract by paying compensation to the husband and go over to the man after her heart. She thus gets back to her home, arranges marriage with someone else, pays compensation to the husband in the form of Reet, and goes to live with the new husband. No marriage is legally valid without the payment of compensation or Reet to the first husband.

The origin of early betrothal and marriage is very difficult to trace but certain advantages are claimed for them. It has to be remembered that these people are practically agriculturists and the utility of a wife depends upon her interest and training in household and field work. It is claimed that one advantage of this custom is that the mother-in-law finds it very easy to train her daughter-in-law when she gets her under her disposal at so young an age. She is impressionable then and the training imparted to her is sure to last her for her life. Her services in agriculture can thus be utilized from her childhood. At times in the plains, where the custom of child marriage was once prevalent but has now been superseded by adult marriage, the mothers-in-law complain against their daughters-in-law. They say that they find it difficult to train the grown-up daughters-in-law who have developed different habits and would not pay heed to their advice while in the days of early marriage they could mould them as they pleased. The girl-wife was given instructions in every household and outdoor work and she took part in everything which concerned the family. She could help her mother-in-law from the early years of her life and thus got a proper understanding of every household duty while a wife who came late had most probably been spoilt by too much caressing from her mother. Further, through early marriage the couple live together from childhood and great intimacy naturally develops between them and they are able to understand each other very well which would not be possible for grown-up people. The girl-wife would after some time learn to regard the relations of her husband as her own and a very wholesome and healthy atmosphere would be created.

Such, in brief, are the advantages claimed for early betrothal and marriage. There is some truth and force in the assertions but the drawbacks of early marriage are numerous and outweigh the advantages. The child wife finds life very hard for her. The mother-in-law is not usually, and cannot naturally, be so kind to her as her own mother. It is sheer cruelty to deprive a girl of tender age of the love and affection of her own mother in the interest of a practical training for the benefit of her mother-in-law. It is the mother's care which a child holds dearest in her life and which cannot be replaced by anything. Rudimentary education is also denied to her for her mother-in-law would never care for her education as her parents could. But the worst of it is that the couple are not really so happy as they are claimed or expected to be. Serious differences develop between the husband and wife as time passes and the numerous cases of dissolution of marriage give a conclusive proof that early marriage does not strengthen the marital tie. The custom of Reet could not have existed and prospered if such marriages were happy. As soon as the girl grows up and finds things intolerable for her, her spirits rebel against her marriage. She goes home, arranges an alliance with someone else more to her liking, pays compensation to her husband, and lives with that man. This custom seems to be a very old one and people stick to it because of their conservatism as also because there is no other way out of the difficulty. We may thus surmise that the need of women as partners in agriculture, their services at home, and the necessity of training them in discipline and loyalty to their mother-in-law might have led to early betrothals and marriages. The evils associated with infant marriage are probably responsible for the introduction of the custom of Reet by which a woman may escape the hard lot to which otherwise she would have been permanently bound.

In Simla, Chamba, Suket and Mandi, Chakrata, betrothal customs are similar to those of Sirmur. In Chakrata, however, a few customs similar to those of trans-Giri are found, while in other places cis-Giri customs preponderate. Early betrothal and marriage are, however, a common feature in all these hill areas and there is practically no difference in the ceremonies performed. Early betrothals are common in Kullu too but often the marriages do not take place till the parties are of an age fit to cohabit. Early marriages are, however, not forbidden and do take place in the interior. The betrothal ceremony is quite simple here too. The father of the boy goes to the girl's father with presents. Promises are exchanged. The girl's father agrees to give her in marriage if the boy's father is prepared to give him a certain sum. If the boy's father agrees the betrothal is complete. It is noteworthy that while in Kullu the boy's father has to give money to the girl's father it is not necessary to do so in Sirmur. It is not in every case that a girl's father realizes money from the other side but only those who cannnot afford marriage expenses do it. In Lahul, however, a slight difference is noticeable in the betrothal ceremony. There the negotiations for a betrothal are carried out by the father and the maternal uncle of the boy. The girl is first selected by the parents or by the boy if he is in a position to do it. The father and maternal uncle then take a pot of *chang* (a local drink, made out of barley) to the parents of the girl selected. There they disclose the purpose of their visit to the father of the girl. The mother is then deputed to obtain the consent of the daughter. If she agrees to the proposal her parents also accept it and partake of the chang brought by the visitors. If she dees not agree to the proferred hand the parents refuse to drink the chang which means a final rejection of the offer of marriage. If, however, they accept the proposal and drink the chang it is sent to them on two further occasions and at the third time the payment and acceptance of a rupee settles the matter. The Lahaul custom, though differing in the matter of drinking chang which is not done in Sirmur, resembles the kachhi and pakki betrothal ceremony of trans-Giri. As in Lahul, betrothal proceedings are conducted in Sirmur too generally by the father or the maternal uncle of the boy though friends or other relations too may do it at times.

Throughout the Simla hills, Kangra, and Sirmur polygyny is widely practised. It is prevalent in all the Himalayan tracts as well as in the plains. But the spread of education and a consequent change in outlook has placed this custom at a discount in Hindu society. Such, however, is not exactly the position in the hills for no stigma attaches to a man who has more than one wife. It is not everyone who can afford a wife in the hills where the mere possession of more than one wife signifies distinction and prosperity. The possession of many wives in a tract where the number of males is considerably higher than that of females would seem improbable.

Polygyny is usually practised where there are more females than males. But in a place where there are fewer females this custom cannot be widespread for the majority of the male populace would have to remain unmarried. Thus it is that polyandry is prevalent in Kullu and Saraj, Bashahr, Simla hills, and Sirmur and so even those who cannot afford to have a wife separately manage to do so jointly. Ii is only the rich or well-to-do who have more than one wife. The rich sometimes keep as many as four wives and moneyed men with two wives are quite common. The *Sirmur Settlement Report* (1881) mentions that the majority of Rajputs, Kanets, Bhats, and Kolis were accustomed to keep more than one wife.

The most important reason behind the adoption and continuance of polygyny in the hills was the importance of women as partners in agriculture. In the past it was not possible in the hills to carry out the household and field work without the assistance of someone else. For that purpose Dhialtas or tenants had to be engaged and they had to be paid quite decent sums of money to settle on the lands. Instead of getting a Dhialta or tenant it was cheaper and more useful to get a wife who could in addition satisfy a man's sexual appetite. If the first wife is childless or has only female issues she insists on her husband's marrying another woman, preferably her own sister, or he may do it on his own initiative without giving offence. When the wife is living a comfortable life, according to the tocal standard, and is happy with her husband, she might ask him to marry her sister so that the latter too might be as happy as herself. Or again where she finds that she cannot carry on the household and field work singly she might ask her husband to marry someone else too. All this goes to show that polygyny is not by any means a sign of feminine inferiority or felt as a degradation by the women concerned. Nor is the husband in most cases prompted to take a second wife by an excessive libido but by his first wife's eagerness to shift part of her household duties on other shoulders. The opportunities of satisfying one's sexual desires are so ample that in legal marriage with a second wife the sexual motive plays an insignificant role. Such marriage also becomes a badge of distinction and a sure sign of prosperity in the family, for a man having more than one wife is not only in a better position to manage his household and field work but has very little work to do himself and can entertain his guests much better. Thus it is that he not only benefits by her economically but socially too.

It may seem inevitable that two or more wives which one may have would be always quarrelling and fighting and making one's life miserable. But an examination reveals that this apprehension is not justified by the actual state of affairs. Since it is only the rich who can afford the luxury of many wives the husband has generally at least two rooms in his house. Only the wife whom he would like to have with him for the night would sleep in his room though in cases where the wives have no feelings of jealousy they may sleep with him in the same room. Quite often the husband has a dochhi where he keeps his cattle and he keeps one wife at his house and the other at the dochhi. He lives in the house and at the dochhi and performs his duties towards them. Since the women married him not under any coercion or pressure they generally have good relations with each other and in case differences grow the injured wife may leave her husband and marry someone after her heart. Sporadic instances of jealousy must of course be expected everywhere but where the second wife is brought at the suggestion of the first wife the risk is minimized though, at times, it makes its appearance later. Sisters are likely to quarrel less as co-wives than unrelated women but even the latter pull on wonderfully well. We came across cases in the hills where children treated their mother and their step-mother, who was not their mother's sister, on the same terms and had no reason to dislike her but were rather more attached to her than to their mother. This is of course by no means common but it has to be admitted that on the whole the relations of the co-wives are not so bad as they are generally painted.

The ceremony by which a second wife is taken is quite simple in Sirmur. At the wedding the second wife is made to sit in one corner of a room, the first wife sits in the opposite corner, while a woman with a lighted lamp in her hand stands by each of them. Then the family Brahman or an elderly woman stands in the middle of the room, and he or she joins their hands and they give each other a rupee. The lamps are lighted to prevent the shadow of the one falling on the other. This custom is common in the hills on both sides of the Giri. A similar ceremony is practised in the other hills too.

POLYANDRY

Polyandry of the fraternal type is extensively practised in Bashahr, Kullu, Jubbal, Keonthal, and the trans-Giri tract of Sirmur. It is not peculiar to any particular caste or tribe. Since it is a phenomenon of vital importance it will form the subject-matter of the following chapter.

Various forms of marriage are practised in the trans-Giri tract. The economic, social, and regional factors all combine to determine the form of marriage and we shall discuss below the nature and origin of the forms of marital relationship in these parts.

The ancient Hindu law recognized eight forms of marriage of which four were approved and four unapproved. The four approved forms were: (*i*) Brahma, (*ii*) Daiva, (*iii*) Arsha, and (*iv*) Prajapatya. The four unapproved forms were: (*i*) Asura, (*ii*) Gandharva, (*iii*) Rakshasa, and (*iv*) Paisacha.

Where the father or other guardian of the bride gives the bride

in marriage without receiving any consideration from the bridegroom, the marriage is called Brahma. It is commonly called
Pun marriage now. When the girl is given in marriage to the
officiating priest it is called Daiva and where the father of the
girl receives from the bridegroom a pair of cows it is called Arsh
and where the father gives his daughter to the bridegroom saying: "You two be partners for performing secular and religious
duties," it is called Prajapatya. All these four forms were originally intended for Brahmans but now Hindus belonging to any
caste may marry either in the Brahma form or the Asura form.

Where the father receives any consideration which is technically called *sulka* (bride's price) for giving his daughter in marriage the marriage is called Ausra even though it may have been
performed according to the rites prescribed for the Brahma form.
What distinguishes the one from the other is that in the Brahma
form it is a gift of the girl pure and simple while in the Asura
it it a sale of the girl for pecuniary consideration. The test in
each case is whether any consideration was received by the
father or the other guardian for giving the girl in marriage. The
mere giving of presents to the bride or to her mother as a token
of compliment does not mean that the marriage is Asura. The
Gandharva is a marriage by mutual consent, the Rakshasa is a
marriage by forcible capture, and the Paisacha is the marriage
of a girl to a man who had ravished her when asleep or when
flushed with strong liquor. In fact, the Asura form was permissible for Vaisayas and Sudras but not for Brahmans and Kshatriyas. The Gandharva and Rakshasa forms were peculiar to
Kshatriyas. The Paisach form was regarded as the most debased
and was strongly condemned, All these forms except the Brahma
and the Asura have, however, gone out of use. A passing
reference to them was necessary because some traces of the
defunct forms may still be found to exist. Any class may now
marry only according to the Brahma or the Asura form. Thus
a Brahman may contract an Asura marriage and a Sudra may
contract a Brahma marriage.

We shall now deal with the various forms of marriage which
we find in this tract as also in other states where polyandry is
found. The most common form of marriage in the polyandrous

trans-Giri tract of Sirmur is Asura. Whether this form of marriage by purchase was of Aryan origin or was handed down by indigenous earlier generations is not clear but it marks a stage in advance of the system of marriage by capture, though a few relics still seem to connect it with the latter. In trans-Giri as also in cis-Giri the act of taking away another person's wife whether by force or by mutual consent is called *har lana*, which suggest that marriage by capture must have been practised by these people. Since the dominance of Rajput influence in these tracts, the Kunnindas and then other orthodox Rajputs having held them in their sway, marriage by capture or Rakshasa marriage which was permissible only to Kshatriyas might have been in vogue. The *Simla District Gazetteer* (1904) also notes that "among the higher castes if a man forcibly makes a woman his wife the marriage is called Har and considered illegal, but among Kanets and lower castes it would hold good." One fact seems, however, to have been overlooked by the *Gazetteer,* namely, that the event is followed by a settlement with the husband or his people and unless they agree to free her from her marital obligations, whether after receiving any consideration for it or not, the marriage would, irrespective of any caste high or low, be illegal in case the woman was married. If no settlement is made with her former husband her connection with her seducer would be illegal. She cannot be the wife of two persons at the same time unless they are living jointly. She must therefore have the matter settled with her husband or her new choice would be liable to conviction under Secs. 497 or 498 I.P.C. for adultery and enticing her away. If the woman was unmarried no such difficulty would arise but even then the parents of the girl would strike a bargain as far as possible. *Har* could originally have been possible because of the aggressor. But now, except in rare cases, Har is possible because of the mutual consent of the man and the woman and because it resembles the Gandharva form which was permissible for the Kshatriyas only. We noticed a case of Har when Bhalku and others of Poka village, Paonta tehsil in the trans-Giri tract of Sirmur, took away Noopi, wife of Harnam of Sara, Paonta tehsil. The accused Bhalku and his brothers had struck a bargain for the hand of Noopi with Harnam's brother but neither Harnam nor his wife were agreeable to it. While Noopi was going to her parents Bhalku and others waylaid her by the banks of the Giri and carried her by force to their village. There they made her put on their clothes and ornaments and, since the family was polyandrous, kept her as a common wife. The aggrieved husband had to move the authorities for redress. We thus find that the working of their social customs and practices suggests that marriage by capture as also by mutual consent may have been common there. The carrying of guns, the beating of drums, and the firing of shots in a marriage, which give it a warlike picture, suggest that marriage by capture preceded the present form of marriage by purchase.

The essential and binding part of the marriage ceremony among the Hindus consists of the *phera* (circumambulation of the sacred fire) which is held to imply the consummation of the vows in the presence of *agani* (fire) and the other sacrificial gods. This ceremony had been held important according to the Hindu law. The Brahma or Pun marriage has come to be associated with it and it is considered odd to accept any consideration while giving away a girl in marriage according to the phera. Formerly marriage was not at all performed according to the orthodox Hindu custom. The phera marriage was all but unknown in the trans-Giri tract of Sirmur. Things have now changed and it is found that the well-to-do and respectable Kanet and Bhat families perform the phera ceremony.

This has been due to their contact with the cis-Giri people and those of Nahan and other areas. In order to raise themselves from their inferior position and to prove that they are of the same status as the Rajputs and Brahmans of the plains they are now everywhere gradually adopting this custom. The Kanets and Bhats living just on the other side of the Giri river have customs more of the cis-Giri than the trans-Giri type. In the cis-Giri, however, phera is a necessary custom and even Kolis observe it. Some of the Koli families of the cis-Giri would not marry except according to the orthodox phera ceremony,

In the trans-Giri tract of Sirmur we find three types of

marriage: (*i*) phera, (*ii*) Jhajrah, and (*iii*) Reet. These types, with slight changes, are prevalent throughout the Himalayan tract under consideration. In Bashahr they are called: (*i*) Biah or regular marriage, (*ii*) Jhajrah, and (*iii*) Gadar or Paraina; in Kullu (*i*) Brahma, (*ii*) Arsh or Asura and (*iii*) Gandharb; in Chamba (*i*) Biah, (*ii*) Jind-Phuka or Gandharb, and (*iii*) Jhanjarira or widow marriage. Though some differences are found in the ceremonies the main types resemble one another. We shall see how these resemble or differ from the forms of marriage in other polyandrous tracts like Chakrata, Kullu, and Lahul. Phera marriage is a recent innovation in this territory but the most common form of marriage is the Jhajrah. The term *Jhajrah* is used for the marriage of a widow in Kangra and Kullu as well as in Chamba. Apparently the term means "putting the *nath* (nose-rising) in the bride's nose" but in Kullu and Kangra it stands for widow marriage. But in the trans-Giri territory of Sirmur regular marriage is termed Jhajrah, in contradistinction to Reet. After the betrothal the bridge-groom's father (or in his absence some near relative) goes to the bride's house with a pundit and a barber and two or three other persons, the number of persons being three or five or at the most seven taking with him a nath and as many ornaments as he can afford. Among the Kanets and Bhats gold ornaments like nath and murki and silver ornaments like dandiyan, jhummack, sis-phul, janjir, har, mala, tandru, paploche, dulri, and bulyan are presented. The nath is an indispensable ornament, while it rests with the bridegroom's father to offer in addition any of the above-mentioned orna-ments. The Kolis and other low castes were not allowed by society to use any gold ornaments, especially the nath. The bridegroom's father and his party are very cordially treated by the bride's people. An auspicious moment is selected by the pundit when he recites the mantras and in certain places near the Giri, women sing the wedding songs. The Shant ceremony takes place a day before the bridegroom's relatives reach the bride's place. A pujan is held at this time and whoever wants to present anything to the bride at that time can do so. Her maternal uncle presents her with a complete suit of

clothes, a *thali*, and a *lota*. Failing her maternal uncle, her
father gives these articles to her. The bride is asked to sit
before the *thapa* (quaint lines drawn with cow-dung on a
wall) and five seers of grain placed in a vessel. Pujan takes
place and the pundit recites some mantras or incantations.
This ceremony is called *sohag lagana*. After the sohag ceremony
or putting on the nose-ring they sing songs and perform
their native dance or gee. The pandit reciting the mantras
puts the nath in the bride's nose, a paranda or mauli is tied
round her wrist, and *gur* or *shakkar* (raw sugar) is distributed among those present on the occasion. It is then decided
as to how many men should accompany the *jhajri* (bride) so that
arrangements could accordingly be made for them by the bridegroom's people. The bride clad in a red garment follows the visitors to her husband's place accompanied by the pundit, barber,
and the *jhajroos* or *baratees* (wedding guests). Ordinarily the
jhajri goes with the jhajroos or her relatives and friends. When
she reaches her husband's place she stays in her husband's
village with her own people and dines with them till the Ghrastni
ceremony which is performed only at an auspicious moment.
Generally the jhajri and the jhajroos reach the bridegroom's
place in the evening when a *dham* (feast) awaits them. At
times the bride reaches in the morning and the jhajroos follow
in the evening. If, however, a death occurs in the village
or some other accident takes place the jhajri is sent to her
husband's place and the jhajroos go there after about 10 or
15 days and then the ceremony takes place. In the cis-Giri
and in Nahan the bridegroom and the bride are commonly
carried in palki or doli. But it is to be noted that in the
trans-Giri the bridegroom's father or some other relative goes
to fetch the bride and not the bridegroom himself. The bride,
when she comes to her husband's house, comes on foot and not
in a doli or palki as is the custom elsewhere. If she is of
very tender age she is carried on a man's back and in case
she is a child her mother goes with her to suckle her. The
Sirmur Gazetteer states that it is counted as an ill omen to
go in a palki or doli in this tract because it is only the
dead that are so carried although this could not be corroborated

by investigation. The bride enters her husband's house at
an auspicious moment fixed by the pundit when a pitcher of
water is placed and Swastikas are painted on the walls and
a *diwa* (earthen lamp) is put near a place called thapa. A
raised square platform is made of each about two inches
high on which turmeric and small images are placed in the
centre. The bride and the bridegroom sit in front of the platform and incense is burnt. The whole affair is managed by
the pundit (Bhat) who gets one rupee and four annas as his
fee besides four or five seers of grain. The bride takes her seat to
the left of the bridegroom. The nuptial knot is symbolized
by tying some part of the dress of the bride with the shirt
or turban of the bridegroom. Both are made to stand up
and *gath-jora* (union of knots) is tied to unite them for ever.
They now change sides and the husband comes to the left.
This is the only phera that was known to these people before
the regular phera ceremony was introduced. Gur or shakkar
is then given to the bridegroom by the pundit. The bridegroom puts it in the bride's hand and she eats it. Next gur is
given to the bride who gives it to the bridegroom who also
takes it. This completes the marriage ceremony and the custom
is called *Ghrastni*. Gur or shakkar is also distributed among those
present. We may note in passing how the gath-jora ceremony of
the trans-Giri tract resembles the Lai Lui ceremony of Kullu.
In Kullu, as in trans-Giri, the bridegrooms plaid is fixed in a knot
with the bride's *dopatta* (*chaddar*, i.e. head cover). The bride
and the bridegroom are then carried round the altar on which
the worship of Ganesh has been celebrated. This is performed at
both houses and this tying of knots is called Lai Lui. A
vessel of water is consecrated and the *balli* (nose-ring which
corresponds to the wedding ring of Christians) is solemnly
purified. The young couple and the guests, or at any rate the
members of the bride's escort, receive a *tikka* mark on their
foreheads, generally from the hands of the bride. Then follows
the marriage feast which often includes a goat which is killed
for the occasion. A very close resemblance is thus found
between the marriage ceremony, especially the Lai Lui of
Kullu and gath-jora and jhajra of trans-Giri. Reverting to

the trans-Giri Jhajra celebrations, it is found that the Bajgi is sent by the bride's people to all those whom they want to invite at the wedding. He goes to them and informs them of the marriage and invites them to join the function. This is considered a formal invitation. The Bajgi is given some grains by those who are invited and a person who lets him go without giving him anything on such an occasion is considered ill-bred. The relatives of the bride who accompany her to her husband's house fire guns. Such sport is called *mohalla*. The custom of carrying guns and fire-arms seems to be a survival of a time when marriage by capture was the rule. But it is noteworthy that in this tract it is not the bridegroom's people that take these guns but the bride's. In other parts of the state in the cis-Giri territory, in Sain and other places, the bridegroom's party carry guns with them and before reaching the bride's place fire them in sport. They beat drums and blow clarions. Naquaras are played and the particular tune of the music on this occasion is called *Jang and Pholanian*. This custom of firing guns and all those celebrations on the wife's side suggest that the custom may be a legacy of a time when society was matriarchal. The procession reaches the bridegroom's house in the evening and the jhajroos on reaching there take their dinner. In earlier days, at the dinner shakkar and ghee were distributed extravagantly, about 40 or 50 maunds of shakkar, 20 to 30 tins of ghee, and 60 to 70 maunds of wheat flour being consumed on the occasion. This is thus a purely vegetarian dinner. In the morning the jhajroos are served with non-vegetarian diet and huge quantity of rice and eight to ten goats are consumed at this feast. These are no doubt the maximum figures. The non-vegetarian dinner is called *gulti* (meat) and *bhat* (rice). The above figures indicate the expenditure on marriage and how hard it is for the poor to meet the expenses. The jhajroos do not sleep but in honour of the wedding they dance throughout the night. This dance is called *Gee*. Men dance singly or in twos. The *Dholki* and the *Naquara* or *ghara* (earthen pitcher) are played in accompaniment with the dance and the songs. Women too dance and keep very good rhythm with the music. The whole night they dance and smoke hookah. The *neodharis* or *nadharis* (guests of the bridegroom) offer presents to the bridegroom's parents in the morning before the second dham is given to the jhajroos.

This custom, called *Neota*, is of great importance because of its economic significance. Every neodhari gives either two rupees or one rupee to the bridegroom's parents and a *lotku* (small earthen pot) full of ghee. In certain parts it is the custom to give one rupee in return for that which the Neodhari had received from the bridegroom's parents at his own marriage or any marriage in his family which is called *aton* and another rupee which is called *gahon* or *agehun* (advance). In certain parts only one rupee is presented to the bridegroom's parents. No written account is preserved of these presents but the bridegroom's parents keep them in mind for they will have to pay to others in their marriage ceremonies. This custom of Neota is important in as much as it shows the solidarity of these people. The Neota is given so that the money thus received might financially help the bridegroom's people in conducting the marriage. It considerably helps the poor people. Thus it is of economic benefit to the family which has to meet the heavy expenditure incurred in this behalf. The custom of paying money to the bridegroom's parents is called Neota Dalna. It is not necessary that the present must be in cash. It can take the form of grain or ghee. If one feels that he may need ghee, rice or wheat at the time when he will have to perform a marriage ceremony he may present ghee, rice or wheat and not cash. This is even more in harmony with the needs of the people and it is a direct help to them. The maternal uncle is expected to bear the expenses of the morning meal. If he is rich enough he may bear all the expenses of these meals but ordinarily he brings a certain quantity of rice and some goats. The other expenses are borne by the bridegroom's parents.

As opposed to Jhajra or the regular form of marriage there is also Reet or the irregular form of marriage. Reet literally means custom. It is not a recognized form of marriage and is outside Shastric prescriptions. It is never the first marriage in Sirmur in the case of a woman though it can be so in the case of a man. The first marriage of a woman in this tract is always performed according to Jhajra. It is only after the first regular form of marriage that Reet may take place. Elsewhere the people who observe Reet consider it a form of marriage which can be contracted by payment of a lump sum of money. No ceremonies of a Hindu marriage are observed. The payment of a certain sum of money to the father or the guardian of the girl if she is a *virgin*, or to her husband if she is married, is all that is required. This done, the purchased girl becomes the legal wife of the buyer. The price of a woman acquired by this means varies according to her natural dower of beauty from Rs 100 to Rs 500. Sometimes the price in the case of an especially prized woman is as high as Rs 2000. This custom has robbed marriage of its character of sanctity and inviolability and a system of divorce has in this peculiar form come to be widespread. Under its influence all domestic ties have been weakened and either the husband or the wife has got a free hand in dissolving the union. More often than not they are seen to separate on trifling pretexts. It will be found from the above that Reet is more of a form of divorce than of marriage. Its importance has increased because of its effects on the life of the people of this tract in particular and of the other tracts in general.

During the existence of the feudal states in the region one other marriage tie was also noticed, namely, that between a ruling chief or a high class Rajput and his khawas wives. A khawas was generally more than a concubine and she was always treated with respect in the palaces, especially if she be the mother of a son. There were three classes of khawas. The highest was a Kanet maid-servant or attendant of a rani who in the phera ceremony had accompanied her mistress in her seventh round of the fire. The second was a Kanet woman brought into the palace in order to be a khawas. In her case a ceremony similar to the Jhajra is performed when she enters the palace. The third was a concubine introduced without any particular ceremony. It was not necessary that only a Kanet woman could be kept as a khawas. Bhat women were also kept as khawas.

We find polygamy and polyandry both existing in the tract. Since the matter of widow marriage is so intimately connected with the working of Reet and polandry it will be appropriate to deal with it while discussing them.

No account of marriage in these parts of the Himalaya would be complete without a reference to Lahul which lies on the borders of Tibet and where naturally Tibetan civilization and culture have a great influence. The bridegroom does not send any of his representatives to fetch a bride in Lahul but he has to go himself to bring her and perform the ceremonies.

On the day fixed the bridegroom's family and relations go in a body to fetch the girl. The fetching ceremony takes place at night. On arrival at the bride's house the bridegroom accompanied by his companions has a little encounter with the servants of the house who will not let him in unless he has paid them a fee. Once inside, the bridegroom exhibits his gifts. The chang is passed round and all the bride's relatives receive a part of the cake he has brought. This consists of roasted barley flour kneaded into a stiff dough with butter and also bits of the dried ribs of a sheep. Then the bride's dowry is presented which is called *zori* or *istridhan*. It may consist of sets of clothings up to eight or ten, a sum of money, utensils required for her new home, a cow, a hybrid yak, and a pony or two. The husband also gives her a dower called *gotam* which is recoverable by him in case she leaves him. Thakurs and even Kanets at times give land to he held by her for life. By such means her position is made stable in her husband's house and the husband does not have any inducement to neglect her or divorce her though divorces seem frequent. The bridegroom then takes the wife home but cannot enter the house unless he performs ceremonies by which all the evil influences the pair may have brought with them are suppo-sed to be destroyed. The Thapa, or spiritual medium, is engaged to counteract the evil influence of the demons. After invoking the benevolence of the Lama this man throws from top of the house a live sheep in front of the wedding party, and its heart and liver are quickly torn out, cut up and eaten raw, the pieces being scrambled for by all the friends present. The Lama meanwhile proceeds with the reading of the Chos which are calculated to scare away the evil spirits. He brings with him a small pot with dough effigy of the demon inside it. He eventually breaks it and kills the demon in the effigy. Then the party enters the house and partakes of the marriage feast.

Closely allied to Lahul is the Kanaur valley where Buddhism is the dominant faith but where the social customs of the people generally resemble those of the Hindus although the observances bear Tibetan names and the rituals are conducted in that language. Here the marriage customs resemble those of the Tibetans. Brothers marry a joint wife, the Lamas solemnizing the wedding by chanting certain hymns, worshipping the gods or goddesses and sacrificing goats.

It is here that we find a group of brothers marrying one woman only. The wedding is quite a simple affair. One of the brothers, usually the one who is the bride's equal in age, goes with some of his relatives to the bride's house on the day fixed by the Lama. There they are well entertained and the Lama solemnizes the wedding by reciting some mantras in Tibetan after the Tibetan manner. Next day they return to their own house with the bride richly dressed and adorned. On reaching home the bride is cordially received by the mother-in-law. After a religious ceremony the bride's right hand is held by all the brothers who are deemed to have married her. A feast is then given to all who are present and the Lamas and musicians are paid their fees. This marriage is a valid one. The bridegroom's father or the guardian gives a dheri to the bride's guardian. The amount of the dheri is usually high, varying from Rs 100 to Rs 1000. The dheri prevents a woman from going over to another man. It is a sum paid to the bridegroom and must be refunded to him if at any time the marriage ties are dissolved. If the wife leaves her husband and goes off with another man the latter has to refund the amount to the husband.

The Lahulis of Chamba-Lahul have a system of joint marriage resembling to some extent that of the Kanauris. While the bridegroom brings the bride home, his younger brother accompanies the bride on her ceremonial return home which is called Phirauni in Chamba-Lahul, Garnoon-Phernoon in Sirmur and Gauna or maklawa in the plains. The younger brother presents a rupee to the girl's mother and this establishes his rights as a second husband. More than two brothers are not allowed.

While considering marriage one has to remember that the various kinds of marriage from the Brahma to the Gandharva can take place only between those castes who are permitted to intermarry. Thus no Bhat or Kanet, male or female, can marry a Koli or Chanal, male or female. The barriers of caste are held intact and any deviation from them results in excommunication or some other form of chastisement. While marriages between Bhats and Kanets are not uncommon the twice-born Brahmans, Bhats, Rajputs, and Kanets cannot marry persons of any low caste. If, however, anyone does marry, he or she at once sinks to the caste of the lower one. The sale therefore takes place between persons of the same caste and not between a person of a higher caste and another of a lower one. In the same caste, however, one may give his daughter to one who is superior to him in status. One generally wants to marry in a family which is superior to one's own but one cannot get out of one's caste except in the case of Bhats and Kanets who at times intermarry on equal terms.

A study of the different forms of marriage leads to the conclusion that three main forms of it are practised in the Himalayan region. The Brahma form is always held in great esteem and people want to come as near to it as possible. The first marriage in the case of a virgin, in a vast majority of cases, irrespective of caste or creed, is of the regular kind though it may have different names. It may be performed according to Jhajra as in Sirmur, Jubbal, and Bashahr, according to Arsh, Asura or Gharbiah in Kulu; or according to Biah or Bedi biah as in Chamba and Simla district. But some religious ceremony is always necessary of which Ganesh Puja forms an essential part. From Chakrata and Sirmur to Jubbal, Keonthal, Kullu, Saraj, and Bashahr with its Buddhist population of Kanaur and Lahul, we find the worship of Ganesh to be an integral part of the marriage ceremony. It will also be noticed that the marriage tie is very loose and is rarely considered to be of a permanently binding nature. That is why divorce is easy and no particular restrictions are attached to it. How the system of divorce under the name of Reet works and affects these people will be seen to hereafter. The facility of divorce on flimsy pretexts and subsequent remarriage which is not at all considered disreputable, together with other regional factors, have affected the morals of the people.

Reet is an institution which serves as marriage to some and divorce to others or again simply as marriage to some or remarriage or widow remarriage to others. It is a very complex custom and needs consideration from various angles. Divorce is not known to the traditional Hindu law for the reason that a marriage, from the Hindu point of view, creates an indissoluble tie between the husband and the wife. Neither party, therefore, can divorce the other unless divorce is allowed by custom in a particular community or tract. Exactly the same state of affairs is found in other parts of the Himalayas as also in the trans-Giri tract of Sirmur where the difference in the number of widows and widowers is thus easily explained.

Reet has been traced by some people to the custom of forcible capture or marriage of a woman by a Rajput, called Har in the hills and Rakshasa according to the Hindu law. But mutual love resulting in elopement of the woman, backed by her economic importance, may have prevailed upon society in giving her a release from her previous husband if she recompensed him for his loss and in this manner divorce may have been introduced to facilitate the working of society. Some people, however, trace it to *karewa*, a form of widow remarriage. Karewa appears to be an off-shoot of levirate. According to levirate, it is only the deceased husband's brother who marries his brother's widow and looks after her. But when the husband dies without leaving a brother his nearest cousin may condescend to look after her and marry her. Even greater laxity is allowed to her and failing a cousin of her husband she may marry any man from the same village or community. It is a custom which is prevalent practically throughout Punjab and even in other parts of India. In castes which practise karewa, a widow, after her remarriage, would almost invariably live for the rest of her life with her second husband. If he also dies she would rarely remarry and would remain a widow. But the women of the hills very often could not pull on with their husbands. The independence which they had gained in return for their services gave them the inducement and opportunity to look for a change. They would always find someone who would be prepared to marry them and compensate the husband. This fact and their importance in the house and on the field kept them always in demand. In the cis-Giri and other parts the common blessing which a married woman receives at the hands of elders is *budh sohagin*, i.e. get old as a married woman. A Hindu woman cares for nothing more than the life of her husband. He is her protector, lover, and all that is dear to her. Her status and prestige in the house are derived from him and with his death she loses practically everything. Strictly speaking, she has to give up all her interest in the material world and shun all worldly enjoyments. A widow is considered to be a most unfortunate woman. She is even considered inauspicious and cannot, for example, perform many of the ceremonies at the time of the marriage of her sons simply because she is a widow. The greatest blessing, therefore, which can be given to a Hindu woman is budh sohagin. The women of the hills are, however, not content with merely getting old in their capacity as married women. Their ideas of married life are different. The blessings which they expect from one is not budh sohagin but *sada sohagin* (remain a married woman for ever). In other words, they want always to enjoy the status of a married woman right up to their death and, if widowed, would regain their status at their will. This may as well be a relic of the times when polyandry was in vogue in practically the whole of the Himalayas and, since several brothers had a joint wife who could not be a widow so long as even one of the whole lot remained alive, this blesssng may have been literally true in a majority of cases.

The prevalence of child marriage is also said to be at the root of this custom. As we noted before, the result of child marriages in many cases is that the husband and wife cannot get on with each other and daily quarrels and troubles make family life impossible. As the girl-wife comes of age and finds things intolerable she goes to her parents' home and refuses to return to her husband. The parents too need someone to help them in the management of their affairs and so they do not resent a helping hand. She remains there for some time and enjoys herself. The poor husband, deprived of the services of his wife, not only finds life miserable but cannot manage his agricultural operations. He married her in expectation of her services on the field and in the house and with her departure the need for a helping hand is renewed. He has two courses open to him. He may either induce her to come back or marry someone else. He cannot recover her because she is not prepared to live with him and he cannot marry again because he has no money. The only course left for him therefore is to come to an agreement with her and renounce his claim over her in return for some compensation. Thus a means is devised whereby divorce comes to be sanctioned by society. The wife goes to her parents, arranges marriage with another, pays the compensation to the first husband, and starts living with the second. This payment of compensation determines the dissolution. It thus serves as a divorce for the first husband and a marriage for the second. There is no other form of divorce except this. It is performed according to Reet which, as noted before, acts as marriage, divorce or widow remarriage as the case may be. If any of the parties finds his or her partner unbearable because of some other reason he or she asks her or him to dissolve the marriage. Sexual morality is commonly lax in the hills and if one comes to detect it in the other divorce according to Reet is the only way out. If the husband finds that his wife does not act according to his wishes or if the wife in turn finds that her husband has no respect for her wishes they decide to part and the wife goes home and arranges another marriage after paying Reet. There is also a rupture when a wife does not get sufficient clothes and ornaments. A hill woman is very fond of them. She asserts that if, in spite of her hard work in the house and on the field, her husband cannot supply her with plenty of clothes and ornaments she is not prepared to live with him. Quarrels between the relatives of the husband and wife also result in the dissolution of the marriage of the couple. In such circumstances the woman is asked by her parents to stay with them and marry someone else. The wife's relations scarcely persuade her to return to her husband. They arrange for Reet with her husband and let her marry again. Physical unfitness is also the cause of dissolution. Where the

husband suffers from leprosy, insanity, or some other incurable
disease the wife has the option of marrying another man though
Reet has to be paid. She has however every facility extended
to her in case the husband suffers from physical unfitness. We
came across a case in Pachhad where a young Koli boy about 25
years old was in the grip of Bright's disease. In spite of all the
medical aid which the poor boy could get he could not regain
his health and was unfit to discharge his duties as husband towards his young wife. His parents did all they could for the
unhappy wife and gave her all the clothes and ornaments which
a woman of that class values. For a time she tolerated every
thing but then, having despaired of his health, she went to her
parents and told them she wanted to be relieved of her husband
so that she could find another who could properly keep her as
a wife. I happened to be present when the final bargain was
struck between the parties. The husband, the wife, their parents,
and other close relations and a Panch were all there and the
matter was put before the gathering. The girl's father narrated
the awkward situation in which he had been placed. He did not
relish severing his connections with the family but could not
help it in face of the troubles of his daughter. She narrated her
story and then her husband was asked if he had to say anything.
The poor boy loved her and did not want to part with her and
said he wanted to have her as his wife till he lived. He was well
aware of the misery that his illness had caused her but, in order
not to lose her, he went to the extent of suggesting that he
would not mind any laxity on her part if she continued to live
with him. The girl and her parents did not agree to this and
finally the boy accepted Rs 240 as Reet.

One fact which has to be noted in the working of Reet in
Sirmur is that it is always the privilege of the husband to accept
Reet or not. No Reet can take place without the husband being
a consenting party to it. The consent of the woman, however, is
not essential and she can be given away in marriage according
to Reet even if she does not want it or agree to it. I saw a
Dumra woman in Pachhad entreating her husband not to give
her in Reet to another. She implored him not to part with her
but to let her serve him and his family all her life. But the fellow

was adamant and since the law was in his favour he gave her away in marriage and accepted the Reet.

After the death of her husband a woman can contract another marriage according to Reet. If the husband has any brother she is passed on to him as wife. If his brother does not want to keep her as his wife, which is unusual, she can marry any other man and pay him the Reet. When her husband has no brother and she has small children she might choose to stay where she is to bring them up. But if she cannot get on with her sons when they come of age she may leave the house and remarry. When the child is very small she may take it with her to the second husband, rear it, and send it back when he has grown up. Whether a child is to return to her former husband or not is decided at the time of settling Reet and if it is not to be returned its price is taken into consideration at the time of fixing the Reet.

It is interesting to come across this particular form of marriage called Reet in this Himalayan region. Many authorities have treated it as a form of marriage but one finds no essential feature of marriage in it. When we take the whole region of the Himalaya into consideration where this custom prevails it may appear to be a form of marriage. But when we consider only the trans-Giri tract or even the whole of Sirmur we cannot take it as a form of marriage. In Kangra district, Bashahr, Kullu and Saraj, Lahul, Jubbal, and Koomharsain it might be treated as a form of marriage. But in Sirmur, especially in the trans-Giri tract, though the custom is in all other respects the same as in other parts of the region, it differs on a vital matter which points to its being a form of dissolution rather than marriage. While Reet marriage in other parts of the region can be contracted by paying from Rs 100 to Rs 500 or even Rs 2000 to the guardian of the girl if she is unmarried or to her husband if she is married, in Sirmur an unmarried girl cannot be married according to Reet. We have stated that Pun marriage is not very common and the parents of a girl receive some compensation for bringing the girl up in the case of Kolis and Dumras and other low castes while the Kanets and Bhats receive it only as marriage expenses. But the first marriage of a girl is always

performed according to the Jhajra even in trans-Giri. There can
be no Reet marriage in the case of a virgin in Sirmur. That is
where Reet in Sirmur differs from the custom in other parts.
Though the bridegroom or his guardian may pay some money
to the bride's father at the time of her first marriage, it is never
done according to the Reet but it is called Patta. It is not every-
body who receives the sum, which is given to defray the marriage expenses, but even those who do cannot receive any sum
more than Rs 24 for this purpose. This sum can be anywhere
between Rs 4 and Rs 24. No father or guardian of a virgin
could thus receive more than Rs 24 at her first marriage and
this payment is called Patta. One may secretly receive a higher
sum but it is considered highly undesirable and if one does so
he may incur the displeasure of his caste and may have to pay
for it. But even when Patta has been received the marriage is to
be performed according to Jhajra. After a Jhajra marriage a
woman may contract as many marriages according to Reet as
she pleases. A man can have a wife by Reet at his first marriage
but a woman cannot marry for the first time according to Reet.
A man too does not like to marry for the first time according to
Reet and would prefer a Jhajra marriage but if no virgin girl is
to be had he has to content himself with one by Reet.

When for any of the reasons indicated above the couple
cannot pull on they decide to break off and the wife goes back
to her parents. If a rapproachment is possible the latter may
try it; otherwise it is announced by them that their daughter
has given up her husband and is prepared to marry again. The
parents in a majority of cases do not offer the girl any sane
advice in the matter. On the contrary, very often they help her
in this dissolution and remarriage. If no one comes for her
hand her father or brother, some maternal relation and a responsible man of the village go to her husband and ask him to
fix the sum of money he is prepared to accept as Reet for his
wife. They would then come and announce the sum agreed
upon. In case no one is willing to pay that sum her parents ask
her husband either to keep her or give her a maintenance or
reduce the Reet money. When it is announced that she is prepared to remarry and a suitor makes his appearance he has to

offer Rs 2 to the woman in her parents' or brother's presence. If she consents to become his wife, after consulting her parents or brother, she accepts this sum which is called *Sotha* or *Dwas*. If the husband has not already fixed the Reet for her the suitor would name the amount of Reet money he is prepared to pay and if the amount demanded exceeded that sum he would withdraw his suit. After receiving the Sotha or Dwas her father or brother, some relation from her mother's side, and a respectable man go to her husband. If the husband wanted to get rid of the woman he would fix a reasonable figure and if it tallied with the amount undertaken to be paid by the suitor the matter would be settled. A day would be fixed when he would be paid the Reet money. Word would be sent to the suitor that his suit had been accepted and that he was to send money by a specified date. When the money arrives the ornaments that were given to her by her first husband are taken off from her person and given back to him. But the ornaments and other articles given to her by her father, brother or any other relative on her father's or mother's side are kept by her as they form her *stridhan* and are not returned to him. Her father or brother and one or two respectable men take the money and ornaments to her husband. They return his ornaments to him. The price of vessels that were given to her in dowry is deducted from the Reet money at the rate of Re 1 per vessel. If any money was given to her in cash at the time of marriage that too is deducted. After deducting all such sums the balance is paid to the husband. He now gives a receipt for the total sum, inclusive of the money deducted, and this receipt is commonly called *Bhar Pai*, i.e. full payment of consideration. They now return home and ask the suitor to come to take the woman. He comes with a pundit and brings ornaments like nath and some clothes. On an auspicious day she puts on the nath and a paranda is tied round her wrist. She is then taken to her second husband's house either on foot or on a man's back but in cis-Giri in a doli. On reaching there gur or shakkar is distributed but no phera ceremony takes place. Sometimes, though rarely, Ghrasni is also performed. Sometimes a feast is also given, as in Jhajra, but on a much smaller scale. She now becomes a legal wife and lives as such so long as she wants to live with her new husband, the slightest provocation giving her cause to leave him for another.

But in this connection it may as well be noted that it is not always that the woman has to do the job of finding a suitor and then accept the Dwas. What really happens in most cases is that the woman had already formed an intimacy with some neighbour to her liking and had obtained his promise to marry her if she left her husband. Even the parents are all the time aware of it and do not often discourage her. On the strength of his promise she goes to her parents and after announcing her intention to remarry accepts Dwas from her suitor and thus tries to dissolve her marriage. The husband too is aware of the situation. He knows very well that she is not going to live with him as his wife but also knows that someone is pulling the strings from behind and so demands a pretty high price. Many a visit is exchanged to settle the matter and he may still be adamant. A good deal of haggling takes place and in the end he is able to strike a good bargain. If, however, he is not much interested in her he may accept a reasonable price. There are cases when no suitor is to be had or the woman does not want to remarry but does not want to remain the wife of her husband. Such cases arise where the father of the woman wants his daughter to live with him and serve him for which he gives her his property. I have come across cases of this kind which have given rise to law suits filed by the father's reversioners. In such circumstances there can be no question of any Sotha or Dwas but the father of the girl goes and settles the Reet money with his daughter's husband. If he agrees to the same, which he has to in order to run his house successfully, he pays the husband the Reet money he has demanded and his daughter lives with him. Now that woman would be free to marry anyone she pleased because her husband gives her a receipt of dissolution of their marriage and permission to her to remarry. She, however, scarcely marries during her father's lifetime though she may be in liaison with one or more persons at his place but may marry with his permission during his lifetime or at her free will after his death. The deserted husband, however, has to perform certain duties. After receiving the Reet money, called *Zara-Reet*, he goes to the *Patwari* (village accountant) and informs him of the dissolution of his marriage and the amount of money received in compensation.

It is evident from the above that Reet is a contract and is based on custom. In the Simla hills, Kullu, Kangra, Chamba, Kanaur and Lahul even unmarried girls are given in marriage according to Reet. In Bashahr the Reet system of marriage is applicable to Jhajra and Gadar marriages. If a wife wishes to leave her husband the marriage can be annulled by the latter's acceptance of the amount of Reet and a rupee which is called *Ched Karai*. An additional ceremony is also at times performed. The husband gives the wife a small stick, called *dingi*, to break it. If she breaks it the divorce is complete. The ceremony is practised in the upper hills by all castes except the highest Rajputs and Brahmans. A similar ceremony is found among the Lahulis of Chamba. Usually two or three persons are present at the time of a dissolution of marriage. The husband and the wife hold a piece of thread between them and break it by pulling it in opposite directions. It both are consenting parties no money payment is made; otherwise payment is made by the party wishing the divorce and is called *man*. It is an improvement on the custom of Reet in as much as a woman has been given the same rights as a man. While in other hills a widow has to marry her husband's brother, in Chamba-Lahul she cannot be forced to do it and can appeal to the court for protection. The Kanauris have tried to check this evil in their own way. Among them the bridegroom's father at the time of marriage pays a sum varying from Rs 100 to Rs 1000 to the bride's father which is called *dheri*. This Dheri later works as Reet money for he alone can take the woman who has paid this sum to her husband. Otherwise she has to stay with him. In Sirmur, if someone runs away with the wife of another, the husband, if he does not want to retain the woman as his wife, receives Reet money for her. Otherwise he may proceed under Section 497 or 498 I.P.C. against him. He cannot claim any special damage because of this Har. In Bashahr, however, he is entitled to an additional penalty for it called *harkaran*. The adulterer has to pay the husband a penalty varying from Rs 6 to Rs 12 in addition to the amount of Reet. He may get it through the law courts. In case of widows in Bashahr, the second husband is ordinarily a younger brother of the first. No special ceremony takes place. When the widow's second husband is a stranger, it is usual for him to pay one or two rupees as Reet to the first husband's family. This special Reet is called Makhtal. If a man died without direct heirs or near relatives and his widow wished to marry again, it was the custom formerly to pay the Makhtal to the state. By remarrying, a widow, as elsewhere, forfeits all rights to her first husband's property which belongs to his sons, whether by her or by another wife. Her children by her first husband are generally supported by the latter's brothers, if any, whether she remarries or not.

"*The Himalayan Tragedy of Marriage,*" as the late Thakur Surat Singh calls this custom, is a most suitable epithet for Reet. The tragedy is Himalayan not only literally but also metaphorically. Fully conscious of her utility to her husband as a field worker and a domestic drudge, as well as a mother, the woman is the mistress of the situation, for if her husband proves distasteful there is nothing to prevent her from eloping with a neighbour of her choice. She may pass on to several husbands in her lifetime as there is no permanent bond of union between the husband and the wife. The result is loose morals. Women can be very easily tempted and thus promiscuous life originates.

There can be no peace where domestic life is so disturbed, where the marriage tie is so loose, and where it can be dissolved at the mere whim of either of the parties. When differences arise the wife does not take the full share of responsibilities in the house. She is then concerned with her own person and must get all that she requires while she does not properly attend to the household and field work. In case the husband wishes to keep her, he tries to meet her demands and thus incurs debt and consequent poverty.

We have discussed how this institution has resulted in the indebtedness of the masses and has put them in a position from which they do not see any means of extricating themselves.

We may here note that the husband has to remarry if he wants to carry on at all. He has to spend money again and get another wife. But if he has any children by the first wife the second one would scarcely give them a mother's care and they may be deprived of all that a child needs most in this world. The evil results of this custom may be classified under three heads: (*i*) domestic, (*ii*) moral, and (*iii*) economic. We will discuss here briefly the domestic and moral effects while economic results have already been reviewed in Chapter III.

As a result of the pernicious working of the Reet, all domestic ties have become loose and marriage has come to have a very insignificant position in the stability and upkeep of society. While a woman is free to leave her husband at her sweet will she has much liberty in choosing her friends and companions and spends much of the time, which is badly needed for the management of her husband's household, in her idle pursuits. Thus it is common for women to have a rather gay time when they go out to fetch fuel or grass from the jungle. They sing native songs, the Jhoori, Ghoogtu, Nati, etc., engage in singing competitions with their paramours and after having a good time come back home. The slightest pretext is enough for them to go to their parents and torment the husband by depriving him of her services. Her indiscriminate relations may result in her catching syphilis or gonorrhoea from one of her friends which she in turn passes on to her mates. Even supposing that she has no lapses after a marriage we may see how, getting the disease once, she may affect a number of families. In a polyandrous family she may transmit the disease to all her husbands and on getting a divorce from them may do the same to the next family and so on. She would in that way be the cause of the ruin of many families. In the case of a non-polyandrous family too she would pass on the disease to one husband after another. When we remember that she may marry any number of times successively the consequences can be easily realized. Shini of Naini Dhar, Sirmur, Pachhad tehsil, married as many as 16 times. Had she contracted one of these diseases she would have been instrumental in transmitting the disease at least to 16 families. Another woman in Bhatgar, Renka tehsil, had eight husbands in her lifetime. It is not very easy in the trans-Giri tract of Sirmur to find women who have had only one husband in their lives. On the contrary it is common for women to have three or four husbands during their lifetime. When the facts of their laxity in sexual matters and extra-marital unions are taken into consideration one may be tempted to presume that every person suffers from one or the other of these sexual diseases.

It is one of the most common complaints that wives do not stay with their husbands but remain for months together with their parents. The husband has to pay a number of visits to her before he can induce her to come back. Her parents hardly have the decency to ask her to go and live with her husband. On the contrary they welcome her, because, while she helps them in their daily work, some young suitor or suitors may come and lend them their services in the hope of getting her in marriage or at least having a good time with her. Such lapses are scarcely discouraged and some families have earned a notoriety for thus using their daughters. Since the marriage tie is weak she knows she can always force her husband either to accept Reet or go without her services. If she marries another man her first husband can have his revenge or at any rate his compensation for he can proceed against her new mate in the court of law under Section 498 I.P.C. But if she simply goes to her parents and lives there and develops intimacy with men who give her clothing and ornaments, the husband can hardly do anything. He can certainly proceed under Section 497 and 498 I.P.C. against them but since there has been no formal marriage it is very difficult for him to establish his case. All the evidence has to come from the girl's village but none would be prepared to say anything against a co-villager. The poor fellow is thus left without any redress and has to accept her Reet and give her a free hand to remarry. It may take months or even years to come to a final settlement and by that time the husband's domestic affairs are thoroughly upset. It is needless to say that the children of such a union cannot in such circumstances receive any education or training. They are left to themselves and grow to manhood in an improper moral atmosphere.

The social effect of this institution has been no less marked than the domestic. It has affected not only the morals of girls or boys but also that of their parents and of the whole village community. The natural result of such easy divorce and re-marriage as is provided by the institution of Reet is the laxity of sexual relations and the total disregard of the laws of chastity. While making that generalization one must bear in mind that even in the midst of such wide corruption one may find a number of women who have been true to their traditions of chastity and can compare with the best that any society can produce.

In brief, this custom is more responsible for the steadily increasing degeneration of the people than all other evils put together. Under its malicious influence domestic relations have been torn to shreds, marriage has lost its sanctity and society has been deprived of all that makes it a means of civic welfare. It allows too wide a latitude to the people in selecting or divorcing their mates and, unrestricted by any moral scruples, the sexual instinct in them finds free play. A destructive social outlook thus gets hold of the people who revel in it without incurring any moral or social stigma.

CHAPTER FIVE

FRATERNAL POLYANDRY

Polyandry was well established in some areas of Himachal Pradesh and adjoining hill areas of Chakrata. Its influence has, however, been to a considerable extent reduced on account of the growth of individuality and the changed social outlook. But in spite of these factors it has not lost its hold on the life of the people and it is worthwhile considering the functions which the institution serves.

It is not easy to determine at what stage this institution made its appearance but it is mentioned in both Vedic and post-Vedic literature. Briffault has shown how polyandry was practised by the Indo-Aryans and other Aryan races such as the Medes.[1] According to him, "the Vedic family was constituted in the same manner as other polyandrous families." The *Rig Veda* and *Atharva Veda* supply ample evidence to that effect. The Maruts are pictured as united to a common bride and Rodasi, who was devotedly attached to her husbands, probably lived with them by turns.[2] Again, we find that a wife is exhorted to perform her duties towards her husband's brothers and to love them.[3] The marriage of the five Pandava brothers with Draupadi is well known. A lady of the name of Jatila is narrated as having been married simultaneously to ten brothers.[4] The Hindu law is of course silent on the subject but it is difficult to find support for the view which is sometimes put forth that polyandry is foreign to the original customs of the Aryans

[1] Briffault's *Mother*.
[2] *Rig Veda* i, 167, 4, 5, 6.
[3] *Atharva Veda* XIV, ii, 18.
[4] *Mahabharata Adi Parva* (Calcutta edition), 551.

for nowhere in the Vedas or the Shastras is there a word of condemnation of the practice though the Aryans must have been in closest possible contact with people among whom it was an established usage. Fraternal polyandry is practised in some Himalayan areas and where it is in vogue it is not confined to any caste or tribe but extends to even the highest castes, ruling families alone being exceptions. Generally, it is only own brothers who share a common wife but first cousins and uterine brothers and at times even strangers share a wife in common in certain tracts. In the Tibetan border marriages in groups also take place as in Kanawar.

We find polyandry prevailing in the greater part of Kanawar and in some places in Rohru of Bashahr. In Bashahr it is found existing in both forms, higher and lower (fraternal and non-fraternal). In the higher form the joint husbands are own brothers and in the lower they are not so. Usually the former only is found in Bashahr but there are scattered instances of the latter too. What happens in the latter type is that at times strangers of even different castes become *dharam bhais* (brothers not by blood but by performing a ceremony by which they become like brothers) and share a wife but in such cases the offspring is not admitted into the brotherhood of his father. It should be noted that, though the husbands are not brothers, the fraternal tie is not lost sight of and strangers can have a joint wife only when they have adopted the fraternal spirit. A dharam bhai is for all practical purposes considered as a brother except in the matter of inheritance. Thus the lower form, which is supposed to allow strangers to share a wife in common, is brought within the framework of the higher form and the fraternal idea is clearly discernible in it. Cousins and half-brothers sometimes have a joint wife. The fraternal tie is thus the basis of the practice allowing them to share a joint wife for as members of one caste, tribe or family, they as possible heirs represent the fraternal group. As a matter of general practice, however, a joint wife is shared by uterine brothers up to the number of six. If, however, there are more than six brothers they get two wives. Quite a number of women have two husbands and some have three or four or even five. The following table from the *Bashahr State Gazetteer* will give us an idea of this as it existed during the earlier times.

Caste	Number of women having				Total
	2 husbands	3 husbands	4 husbands	5 husbands	
Brahman	96	7	—	—	103
Koli	176	48	16	7	247
Jad (Buddhist Kanet)	7	—	2	2	11
Kanet	521	173	68	42	804
Lohar	29	1	—	—	30
Rajput	13	—	—	—	13
Tarkhan	23	9	—	—	32
Total	865	237	86	51	1240

Thus out of a total of 1,240 women who have more than one husband, as many as 865 have two husbands, 237 three husbands, 86 four husbands, and 51 five husbands. From this table it appears that the most common practice is for women to have two husbands though a woman may have three or more husbands. As only brothers can own a wife jointly, the number of husbands is limited by the number of brothers in a family. As four, five, or more brothers are not common, a woman usually has two or three husbands only.

In this tract a form of group marriage coupled with polyandry is found. Instances of a group of brothers marrying a group of sisters jointly are not unknown and at times when the joint wife is barren her sister is brought in as the second wife and thus polyandry, polygyny, and group marriage exist in combination.

The ceremony of a polyandrous marriage is simple. Formerly it was the practice to capture the bride. She would be waylaid, a struggle might take place, and her captors would bring her home. If she managed to slip out of their hands she would boast of it all her life and would be very proud of her achievement. The brothers would in that case negotiate for her marriage with her parents. They would send a deputation to settle her price. The marriage ceremony is completed by her washing the feet of all the bridegrooms and the bridegrooms tying round their caps pieces of muslin cloth called *paju*. The formality of capture is not, however, generally observed now and the brothers or their friends start negotiations with the parents of the bride and bring her home after paying the price.

Conventional methods exist in this region for ascertaining the social paternity of a child. It is usual to recognize all the husbands as the fathers of each child. The eldest brother is called *teg babach* (elder father) and the others *gato babach* (younger father). In practice, however, the eldest brother, so long he is alive, is spoken of as the father of all the children by the common wife. In case the joint family is broken up the wife names the fathers of the various children. The lower classes of Bashahr have sometimes a slightly different manner of determining paternity. The husbands cast lots for the children and thus determine paternity.

At times one of the several brothers sharing a common wife brings a separate wife for himself. If the new wife agrees to be shared by all the brothers no difficulty arises. If, however, she refuses to be the common wife of all the brothers the joint property has to be partitioned. She and her husband have to separate and start a new establishment. Her husband does not, however, lose his right in the joint wife but as a general rule she severs her connection with him. The partition of property is made in accordance with customary rules of inheritance which will be described later.

The Lahulis think that polyandry prevents the division of estates and that is probably why they are strongly attached to the custom. Sir James Lyall describes a case which came before him in which one of the two brothers having a common spouse wished to marry a separate wife. He was devoted to the girl and had even an illegitimate child by her. The common wife of the family, however, strongly objected to this union, claiming both the brothers as husbands and refusing to admit another woman into the household. Her wish eventually prevailed and her husband could not marry the girl. When two or more brothers have a common wife, one of the brothers may bring another wife but if he does so without the consent of the common wife and the brothers he will have to forego his rights in the common household and shall have to live apart with his new wife. He does not, of course, lose his share of the ancestral property.

In polyandrous families, especially of the subordinate land-holders, all sons are considered entitled to equal shares of their father's holdings although in practice they hardly divide but live with wife, land, house, and cattle in common. They recognize the utility of the custom and defend it on the ground that their holdings are too small to divide and that it is impossible for sisters-in-law, with separate husbands and families, to pull on together in a joint family while two or more brothers with a common wife can pull on very well.

In Lahul the sons succeed to the father's property as usual. On the death of a brother the other brothers living jointly with him inherit his property. Any brother living separately from the joint family gets no share in the property. If there are no brothers living their sons would inherit but in default of sons even a daughter succeeds to her father's whole estate in preference to nephews or other male kinsmen, provided that before her father's death she is not married and settled on her husband's holdings away from home. If she is married and is living with her father she inherits his property, and if unmarried, she can hold it for life as a maid. Even where she inherits as a virgin she may marry at any time and live at home with her husband. If she goes away to her husband's home to live there away from her home she may have to lose the estate. Thus even a daughter, as long as she is unmarried or only resides in her father's house with her husbands after her marriage, inherits her father's property in preference to the other male heirs.

The Lahulis of Chamba have a modified form of polyandry. After the marriage ceremony is performed, at the time of the Phirauni (Gernoo Phernoo) or Maklava the younger brother of the bridegroom accompanies the party and presents Re 1 to the girl's mother which establishes his right as the second husband. It thus resembles the custom of distributing sweets[5] to the

---

[5] Anantha Krishna Iyer, *Cochin Tribes and Castes*, Chapter XII, p. 209.

brothers of the husband among the Kaniyans and Pannikans of Cochin. In the case of Kaniyans and Pannikans, when the eldest brother has brought the wife, she and her husband's brothers are seated together and a sweet preparation is given to them which signifies that she has become the common wife of all. The Chamba Lahulis, however, complete the ceremony when the husband's brother presents a rupee to the girl's mother. This is enough to establish his right as her husband. But an interesting restriction which these people have placed on polyandry is that more than two husbands are not allowed. This kind of restriction is not peculiar to Chamba-Lahul. The Bashahr people do not allow more than six brothers to share a joint wife. If they are more than six they have to bring another wife.

The Kanauris, residents of the valley which lying on the upper Sutlej forms a district, Kinnaur, on the border of Tibet, have customs resembling those of the Tibetans. Brothers marry a joint wife, the Lamas solemnizing the wedding by chanting hymns and worshipping gods or goddesses. In the case of Kanauris, it is not generally the eldest brother but one who is more or less the bride's equal in age who goes with his relatives to her father's house on the day fixed by the Lama. The party is well entertained there and the Lama solemnizes the wedding. After these ceremonies the bride, richly dressed and adorned, goes to her husband's house the next day. There she is received very cordially. A religious ceremony is then performed. All the brothers of the husband hold her hand and all of them are then deemed to have married and become her husbands. Guests present are entertained to a feast. The brothers remain in a joint family and have a joint wife and thus the movable and immovable property of a family remains in its joint possession and is never divided.

Polyandry has spread as far as Chakrata in Dehra Dun district in Uttar Pradesh. We are interested in this because the place is adjacent to Sirmur district of H.P. and is separated from it by the Jumna and the Tons. The area in which polyandry is found in Dehra Dun district is Chakrata and in it the tract known as Jaunsar-Bawar is particularly polyandrous. It may be

of interest to note that this tract, where polyandry is still practised on a wide scale, was till lately included in Sirmur. It
originally formed part of the territories of the Rajas of Sirmur
or Nahan. In 1254 A.D. Sultan Muazum Nasir-ud-dunnya-wa-
ud-din ravaged the Sirmur hills. Then towards the close of the
eighteenth century the Gurkhas laid hands on it. On the expul-
sion of the Gurkhas from the Dun (1804) Jaunsar-Bawar fell
into the hands of the British who were aided considerably by
the hill people who harassed the Gurkhas' retreat and cut off
their supplies. On the evacuation of the Dun by the Gurkhas,
it was attached to Saharanpur district and later to Dehra Dun
district. Thus the people of Jaunsar-Bawar are in culture the
same as those of Sirmur. They have the same customs, manners,
ceremonies, religion, and habits. Inter-marriage between the
people of the two areas is still popular and that is probably why
Jaunsar-Bawar has still retained polyandry which is dying out
in other parts of the tehsil.

In Jaunsar-Bawar the husbands are all sons of the same
mother or by the same set of husbands. When the eldest brother
is at home he shares his bed with the wife, and in his absence
the next eldest brother takes his place, and so on. The other brothers have to take their chance of approaching the wife in the
daytime in the fields. A brother may take a separate wife and
may continue to share the common wife also as his own. If, however, the brothers object he has to restrict himself to his separate
wife. He may then separate and obtain his share of the family
property but if in the meantime children have been born his
share is reduced. Some households may have several wives in
common. In such cases the brothers may all jointly share the
wives or they may separate. But even when they separate two
or more brothers may remain joint and may still keep one wife
or more jointly and thus form a group with no further sub-
division. Two sisters may at the same time be married to some
brothers jointly, especially when the first wife bears only
daughters. These people on being asked give the usual explanation that by the working of this custom land does not become
subdivided and quarrels are prevented. On a close examination
we may find that the benefits claimed for the custom do really

accrue from it and it is this strong desire to keep a productive piece of land for agricultural purposes with each family which has helped the continuance of a practice looked upon with abhorrence and disgust by all those who are better placed than them.

The hill tracts such as Jubbal and Keonthal practise poly-andry on much the same line as Bashahr. All these tracts are situated in the interior of the Himalayas and are removed from the plains by mountains and rivers. The Kalka-Simla railway brought some of these areas which are near the railway line within the reach of outsiders. But areas like Bashahr and Jubbal lie in the remote recesses of the Himalayas.

A passing reference may also be made to Ladakh which contains a mixed population of Hindus and Bhotias. Not only do they live side by side but the Hindus at times marry Bhotia women and thus an admixture of blood has taken place. The whole of the country practises polyandry though General Cunningham is of the opinion that the Bhotias borrowed this institution from the Himalayan Kshatriyas among whom it has been present for the last 20 centuries since the Pandava brothers jointly espoused the princess Draupadi. Polyandry of the fraternal type is practised and only own brothers have a joint wife. As a rule only two brothers have one joint wife but two, three, and even four brothers are sometimes allowed to possess one in common. The custom is found to exist only among the poorer classes for the rich can afford to have separate wives and do in fact possess not only one but two or three according to their finances. This practice works as a check on the increase of population and fragmentation of holdings and till lately was not looked upon with disfavour by those who practise it. Things are however gradually changing and a different social outlook has affected its working.

It was suggested by Thornton (1884) that polyandry was universal in Sirmur state while the *Sirmur Settlement Report* (1881) confirmed it to Palwi tehsil, the five Bhojes of Kangra in Majra tehsil, and Waziri Kanyoten in Pachhad tehsil. It was found that women of all castes married more than one husband provided they were own brothers or sons of the same fathers and in special cases only could some other member of the family or an outsider hold a wife in common.

Sirmur state was divided into four tehsils known as Nahan, Paonta, Pachhad, and Renka. The headquarters of these tehsils were Nahan, Paonta. Sarahan, and Dadahu respectively. In the settlement of 1938 Bikrami (1881 A.D.) Paonta tehsil was called Majra tehsil and Renka tehsil was known as Palwi tehsil. Five Bhojes of Kangra formed part of Majra tehsil now called Paonta. This tract was subsequently brought within Renka tehsil and is the home of polyandry. Waziri Kanyoten was a part of Pachhad tehsil in the trans-Giri territory near the boundary of Renka tehsil or Palwi. It will thus be found that according to the *Settlement Report* for 1938 Bikrami (1881 A.D.), polyandry was found to exist in a few areas of the trans-Giri tract, e.g. Renka tehsil, Kangra, and part of Pachhad near the boundary of Renka tehsil known as Waziri Kanyoten. The five Bhojes of Kangra were a big piece of territory. Some parts of it are now commonly called Kangra and are in Renka tehsil while the others form part of Paonta tehsil but are situated in the trans-Giri. At present we find polyandry existing only in the trans-Giri tract of the state and in just a few villages in the cis-Giri near the Giri. It is found in a pure form in upper Kangra while it is practised almost in the whole of the trans-Giri tracts of Renka tehsil and Paonta and in that portion of Pachhad tehsil which adjoins the polyandrous tracts of the trans-Giri areas of Renka tehsil. In other words, we find it existing in those tracts only where it was found to exist as late as 1881 A.D. by those in charge of settlement operations. Though its intensity has been affected, its existence does not seem to be at stake and it continues its influence in spite of being seriously challenged now. We cannot thus accept the observations of Thornton's Gazetteer in this connection and its statement that polyandry was universal in the state has to be accepted with caution. It is possible that it had a universal application here some time in the past but that would be mere guess-work which finds no support from any document.

There is, however, no denying the fact that polyandry exists in the trans-Giri territory of Sirmur and it may safely be said

that it has been practised there for a long time. Those who
practise it allege that it has existed from immemorial times and
the best that can be said of it is that it is not of recent growth.
The earliest reference to the existence of this custom is found in
the *Sirmur Revenue Settlement Report*, 1938 Bikrami (1881 A.D.).
It was found to be practised in the trans-Giri tract of Sirmur,
particularly in Renka tehsil, five Bhojes of Kangra in Paonta
tehsil, and Waziri Kanyoten in Pachhad tehsil. All these areas
lie in the trans-Giri tracts of these three tehsils. The fraternal
type of polyandry was in existence then as it is found now and
brothers or cousins only could share a common wife though in
special circumstances unrelated persons also could have a common wife. We shall now consider if the practice has in any way
changed and the form in which it is found now.

Polyandry is practised by every caste and tribe in this region.
It is common for three or four brothers to have only one wife
but even seven brothers are known to have only one wife. It
appears to be a measure of expediency. The economic factors
are said to be responsible for its institution. Land under cultivation is extremely limited and rocky. It would become difficult
for the family to carry on if partitions were effected and land
divided and fragmented. It would be uneconomical to cultivate
it. Indeed, separate families would harldy be able to maintain
themselves on such divided and partitioned land. It has been
observed that polyandry prevents sub-division of property and
maintains it as an economic holding. It is true that we find a
great disparity in the proportion of the sexes. There are 796
females to 1,000 males. But, as Westermark has shown, mere
disparity in the sex ratio does not explain polyandry and
Rockhill's assumption that the cause of Tibetan or fraternal
polyandry lies in the desire to transmit an estate undivided
may gain corroborative support from the prevalence of the
practice attended by such a circumstance.

It is only own brothers who possess a wife in common
irrespective of the number. The fraternal idea or the principle
of fraternal equivalence seems to be at the root of the polyandry here. The parents of the boy, if they are alive, or one
of his brothers arranges the marriage. A woman is married

with elaborate ceremony only to one brother. She may be married to the eldest, youngest, or any other brother. That depends on the particular circumstances of each case. If they are all at home, a wife is brought for the first time to the eldest brother. But the determining factor is the *lagan* (auspicious star). If the lagan does not suit him, the wife is brought in the name of the brother whom the lagan suits. But if she was in fact meant for the eldest brother, the ceremonies would be performed in someone else's name while she would be considered the wife of the eldest brother. The marriage may take place according to the custom of Jhajra or Reet. It is considered desirable to get the first wife by Jhajra and others by Reet. But whether she is ceremonially married to the eldest, to the youngest, or to any other brother, she becomes the wife of all the brothers and all of them have equal right of access to her. No special ceremony, like that of Kaniyans or Pannikans of Cochin, is performed and she automatically becomes the wife of all the brothers as is the case among the Todas. She not only becomes the wife of all the brothers born but also the wife of any brother or brothers who are born after the marriage. It does not matter when the brother is born. Since he gets a share in the family property with his birth, the principle of fraternal equivalence seems to bestow on him the same privileges in the case of a wife too. Whether the woman was married according to the Jhajra or Reet does not matter. We have said that the wife would be formally affiliated to the brother to whom she was ceremonially married. Ordinarily, it would not matter to whom she was married because she would for all practical purposes be the common wife of them all. But if partition takes place, which is not very common, she would be allotted to the husband in whose name she was originally married. The children too may be called after him. The custom is widely practised and every family knows its working and those concerned accept it as a matter of course. They have no difficulty in imbibing that mental make-up which is necessary for the adoption or practice of the custom. Every child develops the attitude that he is the virtual husband of the joint wife of his brothers. But even if he has not come to look upon her as his wife, those near him may give him the idea. The active part is, however, played by the common wife herself. As the young boy grows into manhood she makes advances to him and thus teaches him to exercise his rights as a husband to her. It is not difficult to induce him to join the list of her husbands for he may be feeling the need of a spouse and before he could go about in search of one, she offers herself as his wife. The whole thing has become so common that it is done as a matter of routine and is noticed by nobody. No formal ceremony is performed when any of the brothers becomes in fact the husband of the woman. Far greater tact has, however, to be exercised in adjusting the relations of the husbands and in not giving any of them a cause for complaint or jealousy. At times the practice is to keep one's shoes or cap outside the room where a husband and his wife are sleeping. That would indicate the sexual possession of the wife by the particular husband. But this would be possible only if a family had two or more rooms and could spare one for the exclusive use of the couple. In a vast majority of cases the husband and wife have to sleep in the same room with the other members of the family. Generally, those who possess separate houses do not practice polyandry but take to polygyny for it is only the poor and the needy who cannot have the luxury of possessing a separate and exclusive wife for each. In a majority of cases, therefore, the wife has to sleep in one room with all her husbands. But whether they sleep in the same room or in separate rooms the wife arranges her sexual relations with them. She is the mistress in this connection. When the brothers have gone to bed she goes and lies by the side of the husband with whom she desires to spend the night. Thus by turns she performs her duties to each one of her husbands. Generally, all the husbands receive equal consideration at her hands. Hardly ever does a cause for complaint arise and however attached she may be to any one of the husbands they all receive equal treatment at her hands.

It is not only in sexual matters that she is dominant she controls the household too. She is in charge of the kitchen. She has to cook food for the family, look to the fuel and grass, attend to cattle, and work on the field. She has also to minister to the needs of her husbands, serve food, mend their clothes, and do all that is necessary for the proper running of the house. If she feels she cannot carry on the duties of a house wife all by herself she may ask them to bring in another wife to share her duties and improve the management of the house. One of the brothers may also feel attracted to another woman and marry her. Such a wife, whether brought at the request of the common wife or by one of the husbands himself, becomes the joint wife of all the brothers and she too has to bestow her favours equally on all her husbands. She is here considered the legitimate wife of all the brothers and even when the eldest brother is at home she must attend to the other brothers equally. A brother who has been away for long receives on his return special consideration at the hands of the wife and the brothers. He is considered as privileged and in order to compensate him for his absence he is allowed to have access to the wife for some time exclusively. As is natural where the principle of fraternal equivalence is practised, every wife is a part of the property to be shared equally by all the brothers. Even a third or fourth wife may be added to a polyandric family of four or more brothers and all the wives would continue to be shared by all the husbands. It would seem strange that they do not allot separate wives to the husbands in such cases seeing that they can afford to do so.

If, however, we remember why they originally brought only the joint wife we may realize why all the wives are held in common. By having separate wives the brothers would render the property liable to be partitioned and fragmented among their respective sons. The sons by the common wife, on the other hand, are regarded as the sons of all the brothers and not of any individual brother. This leads us to the question of the determination of paternity. In Sirmur paternity is determined in a manner different from that of the Todas. The Todas determine paternity by the ceremony of bow and arrow and only the husband who has performed the ceremony is considered the father of the child. If that husband be dead and none of his brothers has performed the ceremony the child would still be called the child of the dead though one of his brothers may in fact be the father of the child. Ordinarily, however, the matter has no importance and if you ask a boy the name of his father he may give you only one name, that of the eldest brother or the brother still living, and if you press him for details he will give you the name of all the brothers. He may not have any particular attachment to any particular name and may show that he considers himself the son of all the husbands of his mother equally. It is only when partition takes place that the determination of paternity becomes really important. In that case a wife is allotted according to the original ceremony performed in her case. The husband for whom she was in fact brought receives her as his share and the children go with their mother. By becoming the joint wife of several brothers a woman gains a life-long married life and becomes immune from widowhood. She is the wife of all the brothers and as long as any of the brothers is alive she cannot become a widow. On the death of one of her husbands she remains the wife of the other husbands. The only difference which it makes to her is that she is deprived of the services of one of her husbands. Where she has been allotted to one of the brothers but no partition has taken place, she may be a widow on paper when he dies but in fact she will continue as the wife of the other brothers of her deceased husband and will become a widow only after all of them are dead. This will also be evident from the fact that on the death of her husband in a polyandric family, the wife does not get a life interest in her husband's property nor do the man's sons inherit him. The property is merely transferred to the names of his surviving brothers who inherit him to the exclusion of sons. As long as one of the brothers is alive the children cannot inherit for in a polyandric family fatherhood is not determined by the biological factor but is a sociological convention. On the death of the last surviving brother alone do the sons inherit their fathers' property according to law of inheritance.

While, however, fraternal polyandry is the common practice in this tract, non-fraternal polyandry has also made its appearance. As pointed out by the *Sirmur Revenue Settlement Report*, 1938 Bikrami (1881 A.D.), even cousins and strangers shared

wives jointly. As far as the sharing of wives by cousins is concerned, it may in fact be merely an extension of the principle of
fraternal equivalence. Since brothers must have equal rights in
every family possession of the wife too must be equally shared
by all. But as cousins are the nearest collaterals and succeed
brothers if they die without issue, they too may be considered
to form part of the same family and the rights which they hold
may entitle them to exercise it in this manner. Non-fraternal
polyandric unions are thus really those where non-blood relations or strangers share one common wife. At times a person
is accepted into the group of the brothers as a dharam bhai.
He becomes their brother for all intents and purposes and performs all the duties and obligations which are laid down for a
brother and exercises all the rights as such. But such a case
would still technically belong to the fraternal type in as much
as the stranger becomes a member of the family and merges
his individuality in the family. Though biologically a stranger
to the family, sociologically he becomes one of its members
and joins the fraternal tie.

But this type of polyandry is restricted to the lower castes
of the hills such as Kolis, Dumras, Chanals, and the like. The
Rajputs or Kanets and the Brahmans or Bhats do not practise
it. In the case of non-brothers the consent of the husband is essential. It is only when he agrees that any one can share his wife
with him but even then he comes as a dharam bhai or adopted
brother. In such a *jori-dari* (joint family), issues born during
the lifetime of the original husband are called his children. If,
however, they are born after his death they are called the children of the husband who joined hands with him. The partner
thus taken is called *ralandoo* (sharer). He may join the family
during the husband's lifetime or after his death. If the husband
is alive he joins with his consent but after his death the widow
may keep him only as her partner but never as a husband. If
she takes him as her husband she has to forego all her rights in
the husband's property. This may seem rather strange but that
is what happens. The widow may not like to abandon her
husband's property and go and live with someone else. The
movable and immovable properties of her deceased husband as

also her associations with the family may induce her not to
leave the home of her husband where she may like to spend the
rest of her days looking after the children. But she needs a
partner not only to share her bed but to help her in the management of her household. She, therefore, asks the persons of
her choice to live with her. The children born of such a union
inherit the property like legitimate heirs. If the widow remarried, she would have no rights left in her husband's family and
would have to leave it. In order to maintain her rights in the
family she does not remarry but asks someone to share her
property and for all practical purposes keeps a husband. She has,
however, the right to dispense with his services at any time
while if she married him that would no longer be possible. This
is the only type of non-fraternal polyandry which is found here
but since it is not based on marriage it cannot strictly be called
so. It is to be remembered also that it is not a very common
practice and only a few cases are found. It is only when the
husband has no brothers and it is difficult to manage his household without taking in someone else or where a widowed wife
cannot attach herself to the collaterals of her deceased husband
that resort is had to a ralandoo. Otherwise the general and
strict rule of the tract is fraternal polyandry though this too is
yielding place to monogamy.

The case of a widow in a polyandric family does not create
any difficulty. It is admitted that a woman is the wife of all
the brothers. She cannot refuse to have connection with any of
the brothers for that would mean a denial of fraternal preroga-
tives. She has thus to accept every one of them even against
her wish. But as a matter of fact this rarely happens. Before
she is married she knows how many and who are the several
brothers of her husband who shall have rights over her. If she
objected to any one of them she would not marry into the
family at all. But in actual practice she is rarely punctilious.
She tolerates all her husbands if she has other attractions in
the house. Otherwise the institution of Reet offers an easy
solution for her. She may attach herself to someone more after
her heart, return to her parents, ask them to negotiate her
divorce, and by paying Reet money to her husband may get

herself released from his family and bind herself to a new one. On the death of her husband she does not become a widow as long as the other brothers are living. They are entitled to have domain over her both on the strength of the principle of levirate as also of polyandry. She cannot, however, be forced to accept them in her arms after his death. She can find a suitor but shall pay Reet money to the brothers of her husband in the same manner as she would have done if her husband were alive.

An important subject of enquiry where several men share a common wife would be whether any friction arises over the uniform allocation of privileges. As has been said before, the wife is careful that all the husbands receive equal consideration at her hands. She is shrewd enough not to bestow special favours on any one husband and thus create ground for mutual jealousy and recrimination. The society too considers it highly improper if she attends to any particular husband more than the others. If this happens still, the husband in question and the wife have to separate and the other brothers receive compensation for the loss of their wife. There is thus little encouragement of any jealousy between the brothers who share a wife. This does not, however, mean that jealousy is entirely absent. A brother may not tolerate the idea of other brothers sharing his wife and may separate from the joint family and get a wife for himself. But this is not quite so common nor practicable. The separated brothers or separated branches of the family have a number of disputes about lands, pastures, and the like and a lot of money is wasted on litigation. Out of the fraternal limits jealousy plays its full part. While a brother does not object to his wife having connection with his brother he cannot tolerate a stranger doing it. The husband resents encroachment upon his rights and if it seems to him that she is getting entangled he may take steps against the seducer or try to remove his wife away from his approach. If in spite of his best efforts he does not succeed in separating them he may divorce his wife and accept Reet for her or may sometimes take the law in his own hands. A number of murders are committed in this way. But it is only in the case of his wife that a man has this feeling of possession and jealousy. He is careful about her chastity, as that is understood in these hills, but much less so where his sisters or daughters are concerned. While he would resent any advances to his wife he does not mind giving freedom to his sisters or daughters.

It is generally noted in the trans-Giri that unchartered licence is permitted to *dhyanties* or sisters including sisters of the father and sisters of the son. They all come in the prohibited degree and so are called dhyanties or dhyaens, i.e. sisters. As long as they are with their parents they have a free time. They can develop as many connections as they like without offending their parents. In the trans-Giri tract we generally find only one family living in one village. The whole village thus presents one solid community linked together by ties of blood. Thus not one of the dhyanties could be had in marriage for she would be in the prohibited degree. But while she cannot enter into a matrimonial alliance with any one she may develop a liaison with one or more of them. Nor is it an offence if she contracts intimacy with a stranger. The reason for this unchecked licence to their dhyanties is that they have no interest in them. But they are as jealous as any other people where their wives are concerned. Disputes about land, forest, and property often arise between brothers but rarely till they have separated. Once separated, a brother would not allow any encroachment on his property or his wife. No tolerance in this respect is discernible and quarrels and litigations are numerous. Whether it is due to the hostilities generated by sexual jealousy within a set of brothers is not certain. But sex does play an important part in their life and it is to suppress the feelings of jealousy engendered by sex that polyandry is generally supposed to have been introduced. It not only restricts population and makes it possible for the poor to get a joint wife for the management of the household and prevents subdivision of holdings in an overpopulated country where land is difficult to cultivate but it also helps the solidarity of the family whereas separate wives lead to disputes between brothers and result in the disintegration of the group. It is argued that any number of brothers can live jointly for number of years but it is not possible for their separate wives to do so for long. The sisters-in-law are instrumental in making their husbands quarrel among themselves. This is what is prevented by polyandry. When the brothers possess a common wife she cannot set one brother against another for in that case she cannot remain the joint wife of all and every preferential treatment on her part may throw her and her favoured husband out of the family. When an additional wife is taken in she will be shared equally by all and so all chances of using the brothers against each other are eliminated.

We have given here a description of the working of polyandry as it was practised in the former Sirmur state. It may be said that Sirmur presents a kind of polyandry based on the Tibetan type and is similar to it practically in all matters. It differs from the Toda polyandry in as much as it is mainly fraternal. With the Todas non-fraternal polyandry has developed and a wife may have to go and live for fixed period with each husband at his place. She has thus to be itinerant according to the residence of her husbands who are non-brothers. The performance of the ceremony of "bow and arrow" determines paternity with the Todas but nothing of the sort is found to exist in Sirmur. In the fraternal type as found here, when non-brothers share a wife with the consent of the husband in his lifetime and merely as a partner after his death, the fraternal idea still holds good. The second husband is believed to have joined the fraternal group and to have merged his individuality in it. He has to reside with the family. He steps into the dead husband's shoes and gets the same rights and obligations as he had. Even then it is a rare occurrence and is restricted only to the menial classes who, due to extreme poverty, cannot otherwise make both ends meet. The working of the institution is thus mainly fraternal and not non-fraternal. An important result which the fraternal polyandry produces as against the Toda or non-fraternal polyandry is that while the Todas practise female infanticide the Sirmur and Tibetan people do not. It is true that in both societies a paucity of marriageable women makes polyandry possible but that paucity is produced in different ways. In developing their polyandrous usages the Tibetans and Todas have not passed through the same series of stages though the ultimate stage of scarcity of women is identical and naturally leads to polyandry. We find that female infanticide has had nothing to do with the scarcity of women in Sirmur nor was female infanticide as such practised here. Stray cases may have happened but the institution of female infanticide does not seem to have been prevalent nor is there any neglect of girl babies. A woman is in great demand and is the mistress of the situation. She is loved at home by the parents and greatly valued by the husband. Her upbringing or marriage does not cost the parents much money. A few clothes of the cheapest and roughest texture suffice for her and she may not be given any ornaments. The question of expenses for marriage or upbringing may not arise at all. As has been pointed out, betrothals take place when the babies are in their cradles and even before they are born. Marriages take place as soon as they are born.

CHAPTER SIX

CAUSES OF FRATERNAL POLYANDRY

Polyandry is usually said to be the effect of an excess of males over females, and it is certain that there is such an excess in Jaunsar-Bawar in Dehra Dun district. There were here only 814 females to every 1,000 males and the excess was still more marked in the birth rate which gave, during three years ending in 1900, only 762 females per 1,000 males. It is at times suggested that polyandry results from female infanticide but there is no trace of this ever having existed in Jaunsar-Bawar.

The Simla district contained petty hill chieftains some of whom possessed a few square miles of land and governed a few hundred souls. Most of the people in these states practised polyandry. Jubbal and the other states which lie near Sirmur practised it on exactly the same line as Sirmur and intermarriages were common. We shall in this chapter study the pressure of population on land and the proportion of the sexes in this area as it was evidenced at the time of the study.

The following table on the basis of the *Gazetteer* (1912) gives an idea about the density per square mile of Simla district:

	Population	*1891*	*1901*	*1911*
	Total	384.2	395.6	385.49
	Rural	204.5	210.2	148.54
Cultivated	Total	—	251.9	2,637.15
	Rural	—	134.6	1,016.23
Cultivated	Total	—	807.0	2,525.3
and cultivable	Rural	—	428.9	973.15

The density of population per square mile of cultivated rural are is 1,016.23.

Coupled with this if we study the proportion of the sexes as given below we may arrive at some definite conclusions.

Year	Actual	Males	Females	Total
1881	,,	23,050	13,069	36,119
1891	,,	22,244	13,607	35,851
1901	,,	26,164	14,137	40,351
1911	,,	24,718	14,602	39,320

This shows that there is a great disparity in the proportion of the sexes in this district while the statistics regarding the density of population per square mile show that the land is probably having the maximum pressure on it. The combination of both these factors easily accounts for the continuance of polyandry in the Simla hill states and we shall at a later stage consider how these factors have kept it alive in the teeth of contrary public opinion. A reference to the available statistics regarding cultivated area and population of the district may also be useful and is tabulated on page 102.

These figures show that there are 24,718 males to 14,602 females out of a total population of 39,320 for the Simla district proper consisting of Kotkhai, Kotgarh, Simla, and Bharauli. For the whole of the Simla hill states we find a total population of 330,850 persons according to the *Census of India*, 1931. Out of this population 171,525 are males and 159,325 females. There are thus 927.4 females to every 1,000 males in the Simla hill states. This is not a marked disparity but considering the fact that in this tract all those who can afford practise polygyny and have more than one wife we may assume that in fact comparatively few males have either to remain single or else to share a common wife with someone else. A marked disparity in the proportion of the sexes is discernible in the other hill states also. The table given on pages 104-5 from the *Census of India* (1931) for the Simla hill states will further clarify the disparity of the proportion of the sexes.

We have left out Sikhs, Jains, Muslims, and Christians because they are in a minority and do not in fact concern us for our present purpose. Out of a total population of 3,30,850 in

Year	Total (sq. miles)	Cultivated (sq. miles)	Cultivable but not cultivated (sq. miles)	Under manured crops—10-year average (sq. miles)	Total Population			Urban Population			Rural Population		
					Total	Males	Females	Total	Males	Females	Total	Males	Females
1881	102	—	—	—	36,119	23,050	13,069	19,299	14,140	5,089	16,890	8,910	7,980
1891	102	—	—	—	35,851	22,244	13,607	18,639	13,251	5,988	17,212	8,993	8,319
1901	102	6	34	19	40,351	26,164	14,187	18,902	13,530	5,372	21,449	12,634	8,815
1911	102	14.9	.66	18.45	39,320	24,718	14,602	24,168	16,995	7,173	15,152	7,723	7,429
District Kotkhai and Kotgarh	—	1088	.49	13.60	10,843	5,147	5,420	—	—	—	10,843	5,417	5,426
Simla and Bharauli	—	4.03	.17	4.85	28,477	19,301	9,176	24,168	16,995	7,173	4,309	2,306	2,003

the Simla hill states as many as 3,17,390 are Hindus and only 13,460 persons belong to the Sikh, Jain, Muslim, and Christian communities. Apart from this the fact is that the interior of these states where polyandry is practised is inhabited predominantly by Hindus and practically none of the other religions is represented there. Towards the Tibetan side, of course, Buddhism is found. We have, therefore, to confine ourselves to the Hindu population alone more so because no other religion except Buddhism practises polyandry.

We find from the table given on page 105 that there are 3,17,390 Hindus in all these hill states and out of these 1,64,029 are males and 1,53,361 females. Thus there are 934 females to every 1,000 males. These figures cannot of course indicate the true state of affairs as they concern those places too where polyandry is not practised. It is only in the interior of these states that we find polyandry. In places which have been brought within the pale of modern civilization by railways, or where education has spread, polyandry is giving way to monogamy for the simple reason that the introduction of railways and modern communications has meant an improvement in the financial condition of the people and a change in their outlook. Where there has been prosperity, polygyny has had a greater scope. We have thus to bear this in mind that in fact there is a much greater disparity in the proportion of the sexes in the polyandrous tracts than would appear from these figures. There are 84,579 married males as compared to 84,114 married females. Married females reach the greatest number between the ages of 20-30, being as many as 24,872, while only 19,200 males of that age are married. The maximum number of married males is 20,902 during the age of 30-40 which shows that the greatest number of married persons is to be found in these hills between the ages of 20-40. The greatest number of unmarried persons is found between the ages of 5-15, being as many as 56,600. Out of these 31,766 are males and only 27,834 females. Out of a total Hindu population of 3,17,390, 1,20,558 are unmarried. That men find it difficult to marry becomes clear from the fact that out of 1,20,558 unmarried persons 70,101 are males and only 50,457 females. The disparity in the proportion of the sexes is marked,

SIMLA HILLS STATES

Age-group (all religions)	Population			Unmarried			Married			Widowed		
	Persons	Males	Females	Persons	Males	Females	Persons	Males	Females	Persons	Males	Females
	3,30,850	1,71,525	1,59,325	1,26,190	73,541	52,648	1,68,693	84,579	84,114	35,970	13,405	22,562
0-1	9,360	4,622	4,738	9,360	4,622	4,738	—	—	—	—	—	—
1-2	7,003	3,432	3,571	7,003	3,432	3,571	—	—	—	—	—	—
2-3	7,848	3,729	4,119	7,848	3,728	4,119	1	1	—	—	—	—
3-4	8,242	3,940	4,302	8,208	3,929	4,279	34	11	23	—	—	—
4-5	8,201	4,008	4,193	8,117	3,980	4,137	81	26	55	3	2	1
Total 0-5	40,654	19,731	20,923	40,535	19,691	20,844	116	38	78	3	2	1
5-10	36,157	18,397	17,760	32,882	17,563	15,319	3,207	808	2,399	68	26	42
10-15	34,157	17,888	16,269	26,214	15,625	10,562	7,730	2,158	5,572	213	78	135
15-20	29,302	14,910	14,392	10,764	8,211	2,553	17,816	6,339	11,477	722	360	362
20-30	58,528	29,332	29,196	9,693	7,731	1,962	45,892	20,067	25,825	2,943	1,534	1,409
30-40	51,019	26,680	24,339	3,257	2,578	679	42,259	21,744	20,515	5,503	2,358	3,145
40-50	36,636	20,017	16,619	1,519	1,146	373	27,360	16,187	11,173	7,757	2,684	5,073
50-60	25,207	13,999	11,208	797	582	215	15,793	10,586	5,207	8,617	2,831	5,786
60 and over	19,190	10,571	8,619	529	387	142	8,520	6,652	1,868	10,141	3,532	6,609

Hindu	3,17,390	1,64,029	1,53,361	1,20,558	70,101	50,457	1,62,211	81,201	81,010	34,621	12,727	21,894
0-1	8,945	4,417	4,528	8,945	4,417	4,528	—	—	—	—	—	—
1-2	6,682	3,268	3,414	6,682	3,268	3,414	—	—	—	—	—	—
2-3	7,489	3,542	3,947	7,488	3,541	3,947	1	1	—	—	—	—
3-4	7,898	3,759	4,139	7,864	3,748	4,116	34	11	23	—	—	—
4-5	7,851	3,822	4,029	7,769	3,795	3,974	79	25	54	3	2	1
Total 0-5	38,865	18,808	20,057	38,748	18,769	19,979	114	37	77	3	2	1
5-10	34,556	17,563	17,002	31,497	16,787	14,710	3,006	753	2,253	62	23	39
10-15	32,619	17,081	15,538	25,103	14,979	10,124	7,316	2,028	288	200	74	126
15-20	28,024	14,230	13,794	10,274	7,844	2,430	17,055	6,042	11,013	695	344	351
20-30	56,099	27,987	28,112	9,191	7,326	1,865	44,072	19,200	24,872	2,836	1,461	1,375
30-40	49,095	25,557	23,538	3,054	2,407	647	40,734	20,902	19,832	5,307	2,248	3,059
40-50	35,297	19,183	16,114	1,427	1,069	358	26,405	15,582	10,823	7,465	2,532	4,933
50-60	24,347	13,467	10,880	755	548	207	15,281	10,233	5,048	8,311	2,686	5,625
60 and over	18,479	10,153	8,326	509	372	137	8,228	6,424	1,804	9,742	3,357	6,358

there being 1,64,029 males to 1,53,361 females but about an equal number of persons of both sexes is found to be married. Thus we have 81,201 married males to 81,010 married Hindu females and the males in excess of the females have to remain unmarried. That is why there are 70,101 unmarried males to 50,457 unmarried Hindu females. While up to the age of five the number of unmarried persons of both sexes is practically the same, being 18,769 males and 19,979 females, there is a great difference in their numbers between the ages of 5-15, there being as many as 31,766 unmarried males and only 24,834 unmarried females. Between the age of 15-20 there are 7,844 unmarried males as compared to 2,430 unmarried females, between 20-30 as many as 7,326 unmarried males as compared to 1,865 unmarried females, between 30-40 2,407 unmarried males as compared to 674 unmarried females, and between 40-50 1,069 unmarried males to 358 unmarried females. This shows that between the age of 20-50, which is a time when persons of both sexes should in fact be married, there is a very great difference between the numbers of unmarried persons of both sexes and males are double the number of females during this age. These unmarried men during this period of their manhood have either to go without wives and live on sexual lapses or to share some-one else's wife and thus never feel the biological necessity of marrying at all. It is true that there is a good deal of sexual laxity in the hills and unions out of wedlock were either rare or odious but in order to get a peaceful life and manage one's home nowhere else is the necessity of a wife more felt than in such places where the household and the field cannot be managed without the help of a woman and life becomes miserable without one. Having neither the means nor the chance of getting separate wives these people have to take recourse to the second alternative and share a wife with a brother or brothers. Nor is it possible for most of them to get separate wives at all for a glance at the statistics shows that there are unmarried females only up to the age of 15 and after that only a few are left unmarried. There are as many as 44,813 females within the age of 15 out of a total of 50,457 unmarried females. There are just a few who are still unmarried after the age of 15 or 20.

Tehsils	Agriculturist			Non-agriculturist			Total		
	Males	*Females*	*Total*	*Males*	*Females*	*Total*	*Males*	*Females*	*Total*
Palvi (now Renka)	13,757	11,949	25,706	9,827	9,120	18,947	27,184	21,069	48,253
Pachhad	10,839	7,744	18,583	6,447	7,149	13,569	17,286	14,893	32,179
Nahan	3,899	2,083	5,982	6,239	5,304	11,543	10,138	7,387	17,525
Majra (now Paonta)	3,973	672	4,645	4,724	5,045	9,769	8,697	5,717	14,414
Total	36,068	24,448	58,516	27,237	26,618	53,855	63,305	49,066	1,12,371

SOURCE : *Settlement Report*, 1938 Bikrami (1881 A.D.), Sirmur State.

Since a number of men share the wives of their brothers all their life and it is only the eldest brother who actually brings the wife who is considered married, the others are considered unmarried for purposes of the census and that explains the great disparity between the number of unmarried males and unmarried females, which is 70,101 unmarried males to 50,457 unmarried females. A reference to Sirmur State (see page 107) in this connection may be useful.

It will be noticed that the non-agriculturists do not have any marked disparity in the proportion of the sexes but the agriculturists have it. The non-agriculturists are not faced with the problem of subdivision of holdings and are generally better off. They are not bound down to the soil and may easily move to any place which offers them a better living but the agriculturists, tied down by their holdings, have to eke out their living there. Out of a total population of 1,12,371 we find 63,305 males and 49,066 females which means that there are 775.07 females for the whole state for every 1,000 males. If we take the rural population of the whole state, we find that out of a total of 58,516 persons 36,068 are males and only 22,448 females. Thus there are 685.05 females for every 1,000 males. Taking the tehsils individually we find that out of a total agricultural population of Palvi tehsil (later Renka) of 29,306 there are 13,757 males to 11,949 females or 688.4 females for every 1,000 males and similarly for Pachhad there are 10,839 males to 7,744 females or 714.4 females for every 1,000 males. In Nahan tehsil there are 3,899 males to 2,083 females out of a total agriculturist population of 5,982 or 534.2 females for every 1,000 males. We however find a most marked state of disparity in the proportion of the sexes in the rural population of Majra tehsil (later called Paonta tehsil). In that tehsil there is a total population of 4,645 out of which 3,973 are males and only 672 females. There are thus only 169.14 females for every 1,000 males in this tehsil. We get the following table for the total rural population of the state as found in 1938 Bikrami (1881 A.D.).

These figures not only indicate that there were far too many males for females but they definitely prove that polyandry was

			Females for every 1,000 males	
Total	*Renka*	*Pachhad*	*Nahan*	*Paonta*
775.07	685.05	688.4	714.4	169.4

practised in an acute form. Nahan was the only tehsil which had more than 700 females for every 1,000 males. Renka and Pachhad had 685.05 and 688.4 females respectively while Paonta had a most extraordinary disparity in the proportion of sexes in as much as it had only 169.4 females for every 1,000 males. This figure appears to be improbable at first sight but looking at the past we do not find it so. In those days the whole of the fertile part of the tehsil called the Doon, which lies at the foot of the hills and extends as far as the boundaries of the Ambala district on one side and Saharanpur on the other, was uncultivated and unpopulated. It was one vast expanse of forest and waste land infested by the tiger, spotted deer, wild bear, and swamp deer. The only inhabited part of the tehsil was the trans-Giri tract of the five Bhojes of Kangra, a thickly populated area where polyandry was practised extensively and which still preserves it in its original form. The polyandry practised was of the fraternal type and there was no limit to the number of brothers who could share a wife. As a matter of fact, the more the number of brothers sharing a wife the greater was the pride of their progeny. It was quite common for as many as seven brothers to have a joint wife and cases of quarrels or jealousies among them were unknown. No offence was taken if another wife was brought. She would be treated as a common wife by all the brothers and her issues too would be considered the children of all the brothers. The children called all the husbands of the wife their fathers. Rarely did a brother separate from the other brothers nor would a woman like to be the wife of only one husband. She preferred a family where there would be many husbands and would not like to separate with one of them from the rest of the family. It was probably due to the fact that she received greater consideration when she was the joint wife of several brothers than when she was connected with only one.

Among many polyandrous peoples there are said to be more men than women and there polyandry has in several cases been directly attributed to this fact. In Tibet it has been said to exist as a necessary institution, meant to check the increase of population in regions from which emigration is difficult and to keep the family property intact. It is further said partly to be due to the dangers or difficulties which would surround a woman left alone in her home during the prolonged absence of her husband. We have now to find out the cause of polyandry in Sirmur and see whether the causes enumerated above or other causes have been instrumental in giving birth to this institution in these hills. The difficulty in coming to any definite conclusions in the case of Tibetan polyandry has been the lack of reliable figures. Unless trustworthy statistics are available it is impossible to formulate precise conclusions. We cannot get statistics for the greater part of the Simla hills. Fortunately, we have some statistics about the population, land and distribution of population in the case of Sirmur state and our conclusions regarding it can be based on reliable data. We have relied on the *Census of India* (1931) and the *Sirmur State Gazetteer* (1931). The polyandry practised in Sirmur is of the fraternal type and does not in any material aspect differ from the true Tibetan type. Though the masses practising it are not Tibetans but Hindus, the institution has not lost its character or altered to any appreciable extent. The conclusions thus arrived at may fairly be considered applicable to the Tibetan polyandry for neither the locality nor the people, nor the practice of the institution differ materially in the two regions and similarity in all the conditions of life ought to produce similar results.

The two most important factors which have caused the adoption of this practice by the people are scarcity of women and a desire to transmit an estate undivided. The latter may be due to the scarcity of land as is the case here. Another motive, that of affording protection to the wife in a dangerous country when the husband is away, is also worthy of note. We shall try to see how far they have worked in keeping this institution alive in these hills.

Whether disparity in the proportion of the sexes is a vital

reason for the prevalence of polyandry or merely a contributing factor may be definitely decided. Risley's idea that no co-relation exists between the disparity of the sexes and polyandry may be true in a society where individual tendencies have a free scope but where such is not the case it has some co-relation as brothers may easily share a wife in such society. Whether the disparity is brought about by female infanticide or by nature the two go side by side and each may react on the other. We find marked disparity in the proportion of the sexes when we examine the following table showing the proportion in 1911 for major castes in Sirmur state:

Caste	Males	Females	Females per 1,000 males
Kanet	22,756	18,928	796.76
Bhat	9,747	8,343	855.95
Koli or Dagi	16,052	13,861	863.50
Dumra	2,881	2,479	860.81
Chanal	1,036	832	803.08

For the whole state in 1911 we had 796.76, 855.95, 863.50, 860.81, and 803.08 females for every 1,000 males of Kanet, Bhat, Koli or Dagi, Dumra and Chanal castes. Punjab gave the following figures in 1921 for districts and states:

	Number of females per 1,000 males				
Sirmur	1881	1891	1901	1911	1921
	775	792	798	822	824

There is a marked disparity in the proportion of the sexes but one noteworthy fact is that the number of females has gradually increased although even in 1921 there were only 824 females for every 1,000 males.

The *Census of India* (Punjab, 1931 Table vii, Age, Sex and Civil Condition, Part B) gives the following figures for Sirmur state.

Age-group (all religions)	Population			Unmarried			Married			Widowed		
	Persons	Males	Females	Persons	Males	Females	Persons	Males	Females	Persons	Males	Females
	1,48,568	82,384	66,184	47,047	28,970	18,077	87,846	47,932	39,914	13,675	5,482	8,192
0—1	3,551	1,830	1,721	3,507	1,789	1,718	44	41	3	—	—	—
1—2	3,439	1,770	1,669	3,333	1,681	1,652	106	89	17	—	—	—
2—3	3,817	1,907	1,910	3,627	1,771	1,856	190	136	54	—	—	—
3—4	3,883	1,911	1,972	3,534	1,701	1,833	347	209	138	2	1	1
4—5	3,839	1,942	1,897	3,362	1,672	1,690	470	267	203	7	3	4
Total 0—5	18,529	9,360	9,169	17,363	8,614	8,749	1,157	742	415	9	4	5
5—10	16,674	8,926	7,748	12,358	6,844	5,514	4,273	2,059	2,214	43	23	20
10—15	15,774	8,698	7,076	9,017	5,738	3,279	6,667	2,913	3,754	90	47	42
15—20	13,900	7,542	6,358	3,270	2,915	355	10,375	4,463	5,912	255	164	91
20—30	28,013	15,275	12,808	2,986	2,868	118	24,016	11,772	12,244	1,081	635	446
30—40	23,197	13,365	9,832	1,108	1,068	40	20,007	11,362	8,638	2,082	928	1,154
40—50	15,223	9,122	6,101	500	486	14	11,752	7,520	4,232	2,971	1,116	1,855
50—60	9,610	5,683	3,927	255	248	7	6,080	4,268	1,812	3,275	1,167	2,108
60 and over	7,578	4,413	3,165	190	189	1	3,519	2,826	693	3,869	1,398	2,471
Hindu	1,39,031	76,922	62,109	42,766	26,239	16,527	83,471	45,650	37,821	12,794	5,033	7,761
0—1	3,230	1,658	1,572	3,186	1,617	1,569	44	41	3	—	—	—
1—2	3,179	1,631	1,548	3,073	1,542	1,531	106	89	17	—	—	—
2—3	3,541	1,761	1,780	3,353	1,625	1,728	188	136	52	2	1	—
3—4	3,611	1,771	1,840	3,267	1,562	1,705	342	208	134			1

4—5	3,566	1,804	1,762	3,102	1,540	1,562	457	261	197	7	3	4
5												
Total 0—5	17,127	8,625	8,502	15,981	7,886	8,095	1,137	735	402	9	4	5
5—10	15,394	8,246	7,148	11,257	6,224	5,033	4,097	2,001	2,096	40	21	19
10—15	14,550	8,021	6,529	8,115	5,169	2,946	6,353	2,809	3,544	82	43	39
15—20	12,928	6,984	5,944	2,909	2,609	300	9,784	4,221	5,563	235	154	81
20—30	26,308	14,235	12,073	2,650	2,551	99	22,667	11,103	11,564	991	581	410
30—40	21,992	12,630	9,362	990	955	35	19,061	10,826	8,235	1,941	849	1,092
40—50	14,448	8,636	5,812	460	447	13	11,206	7,173	4,033	2,782	1,016	1,766
50—60	9,128	5,386	3,742	234	229	5	5,804	4,082	1,722	3,090	1,075	2,015
60 and over	7,156	4,159	2,997	170	169	1	3,362	2,700	622	3,624	1,290	2,334

There are 66,184 females to 82,384 males for all religions in Sirmur state which means that there are 803.35 females for every 1,000 males in the whole state. Looking at the number of married persons we find that there are only 87,846 married persons in the state of whom 47,932 are males and 39,914 females. We thus find that there are 832.05 married females for every 1,000 married males. There are 47,047 unmarried persons in all. Only 18,077 females are unmarried while as many as 28,970 males are unmarried. When we remember that the people stay at home and do not go out except temporarily for manual labour in other areas we can safely surmise that the husbands share wives. The disparity in the proportion of un-married persons of both sexes still further proves that the males cannot in any case have a greater number of females in marriage and it is not possible to have a larger proportion of wives. On a closer examination we find that it is not all reli-gions which show this disparity whether in the proportion of the sexes or in the number of married males and females. The Hindus, who form the bulk of the population, show a marked disparity in the proportion of the sexes. There are 1,39,031 Hindus in all in the state. Of these 76,922 are males and 62,109 females. There are thus 807.40 females for every 1,000 Hindu males. We further find that only 83,471 Hindus are married, of whom 45,650 are males and 37,821 females. Thus there are 828.49 married females to every 1,000 married Hindu males. Since the polyandrous tract contains practically exclusively a Hindu population it is this community alone which practises polyandry. But we have also to bear in mind the fact that it is not every member of this community who practises it in every part of the state. Polyandry is restricted to the trans-Giri tract and there too it is not practised in the whole of the territory. Some of the trans-Giri people do not practise it at all and in cis-Giri in Pachhad, Paonta, and Nahan tehsils, it is looked down upon by the people. What is really relevant for our pur-pose is that it is not the whole Hindu society of the state which practises it but only a few and so the figures for the total Hindu population cannot be correct in their application to polyandry. We shall have to study as far as possible the proportion of the

sexes not only in the whole state but in the different tehsils
and in polyandrous and non-polyandrous tracts. We have also
to consider that Hindu society consists of many castes and
some of them which are found only in Pachhad, Nahan or
Paonta tehsils do not practise polyandry at all. In order, therefore, to understand the exact state of affairs we may in brief
refer to the castes and tribes found here. Castes which number
below 500 have been omitted in the following chart which is
based on the authority of *Sirmur State Gazetter* (Part B, 1931).

Caste	1901	1911	1921	State total 1931		
				Persons	Males	Females
Bhat	16,513	18,090	17,652	9,532	5,722	3,810
Brahman	2,669	2,398	2,562	10,987	6,008	4,979
Chamar	7,085	5,381	5,588	5,852	3,308	2,544
Chanal	1,914	1,886	1,789	1,821	1,093	728
Dhaki or Koli	28,031	29 913	28,921	31,306	16,934	14,372
Dumra	5,021	5,350	3,217	5,438	2,951	2,487
Kanait	40,395	41,684	42,353	41,926	23,306	18,620
Rajput	3,510	3,863	4,494	6,041	3,486	2,555

The Bhats are no other than Brahmans and Kanets are the
Rajputs of the Himalayas. In 1921 there were 2,562 Brahmans
but in 1931 their number rose to 10,987. One would have to
find some reason for this extraordinary rise in the number of
members of this community. A glance at the number of Bhats
may offer a solution. It was 17,652 in 1921 but fell to 9,532
only in 1931. Something of the same nature may also be
noticed in the case of the Kanets and Rajputs. The number of
Kanets fell from 42,353 in 1921 to 41,926 in 1931 while that of
Rajputs rose from 4,494 in 1921 to 6,040 in 1931. What happened in the case of these communities is that many persons
who had been entered as Bhats and Kanets in 1921 were rightly
entered as Brahmans and Rajputs respectively in 1931. This
resulted in a fall in the number of Bhats and Kanets and a
corresponding rise in the number of Brahmans and Rajputs.

A Kanet or a Bhat is so simply because he may call himself by that name. Otherwise there is nothing to force him to have that name. But, as prejudice existed more against the Kanets than the Bhats, greater difference in numbers is noticeable in the case of Bhats and Brahmans than in that of Kanets and Rajputs. It will be found from the table that in every other caste except Bhat and Kanet a marked increase in the number of members is discernible. In no other caste in 1931 is there any fall in the number of its members. Some of the Kanets and Bhats entered as such in 1921 were entered as Rajputs and Brahmans in 1931 and subsequently then the Punjab government also dropped this distinction of Kanets and Rajputs and entered the former as Rajputs in all revenue papers. Bhats, Brahmans, Chamars, Chanals, Dhaki and Koli, Dumras, Kanets, and Rajputs are the castes and tribes which are found in the polyandrous part of the locality and who practise polyandry.

We get the following numbers of females per 1,000 males: Bhats 665.85, Chanals 666.05, Kanets 713.12, Rajputs 732.93, Chamars 768.8, Brahmans 828.72, Dumras 842.76, and Dhakis and Kolis 853.74. The Bhats stand at the top of the list having only 665.85 females for 1,000 males, while the Chanals follow with only 666.05 females for per 1,000 males. This extraordinary disparity in the proportion of the sexes among the Bhats may be due to the fact, as stated before, that many of the Bhats, especially those who were a little more cultured than the rest and did not practise polyandry, entered themselves as Brahmans so that the community was deprived in the calculations of a number of persons with the result that the disparity of the sexes among those who practised polyandry increased. The Brahmans, on the other hand, show 828.72 females per 1,000 males. They have a comparatively greater number of females because some non-polyandrous Bhats had entered their ranks. If we add the males and females of both Bhats and Brahmans we may get the true proportion of their sexes. We find 5,722 males and 3,810 females among Bhats and 6,008 males and 4,979 females among the Brahmans. By adding them we get 11,730 Bhat and Brahman males and 8,789 Bhat and

Brahman females. We thus find that there are 749.28 females per 1,000 Bhat and Brahman males but even this figure is below the average which is 792.97 females per 1,000 males. The case of Chanals is different because they are a small community which consists only of 1,821 persons. They are very poor and their condition remains practically what is was. The Kanets and Rajputs do not show much difference between the numbers of their males and females for many of the Kanets (like the Bhats) were not entered as Rajputs. The Dumras and Chamars are not so numerous as others. The bulk of the population consists of Bhats and Brahmans, Kanets and Rajputs, and Dhakis and Kolis. The Dhakis and Kolis show the greatest number of females, having as many as 853.74 per 1,000 males. No special reason can be adduced for the number of females in this community. All these castes are polyandrous though the practice differs according to the circumstances of each family. The Kolis practise polyandry as much as others though it is a noticeable fact that they are not so strong in physique as the Bhats, Brahmans, Kanets or Rajputs and have fewer children. They are not generally so well-fed as the ordinary Bhat, Brahman, Kanet or Rajput, who are their overlords, and these facts may have had something to do with their having a greater number of females than males. We have shown how a great disparity in the proportion of the sexes exists in castes and tribes inhabiting this area. A word of caution is however needed in as much as these castes and tribes are found not only in the trans-Giri tract but in the non-polyandrous part of the state too. In the cis-Giri they are all non-polyandrous. In the majority of cases in the cis-Giri they are monandric though the well-to-do are polygynous. In trying to find out the extent of polyandry we have to remember that the average form of a family is monandric and it is not every one which practises polyandry. Even where it is practised there is a growing tendency to give it up and take to monandric marriage. All that is meant is that the Bhats, Brahmans, Kanets, Rajputs, Chanals, Chamars, Dumras, and Kolis living in the cis-Giri territory do not practise polyandry and so these figures do not give a correct idea of the effects of polyandry on the proportion of the sexes. We will have to see how exactly the practice affects the proportion of the sexes in areas where it can be definitely located. We may refer to the number of persons inhabitating those areas and draw conclusions for it is clear that practically all the castes and tribes who live in those localities permanently practise polyandry. An idea of the population may be had from the table given on page 119 showing distribution of population. Another aspect of the matter is the pressure of population on land and how a state has been reached when no further lands are available for cultivation and even those that are available have been exhausted and can stand the strain no longer. For the present, however, we shall study the disparity in the proportion of the sexes.

The state was divided into four tehsils: Nahan, Paonta, Renka, and Pachhad. Nahan lies in the cis-Giri territory of Sirmur and is situated far off from the Giri. Nowhere is polyandry found to exist there. We may also notice that the disparity in the proportion of the sexes in this tehsil is not so marked as in others. There is one town, Nahan, the capital of the state, in this tehsil. The urban population is 7,808, 4,584 being males and 3,224 females. The disparity between the number of males and females is due to the fact that many males come to the city for service in the state departments as also for manual labour. Most of them come without their women and so a marked disparity in the proportion of the sexes is natural. In the rural population there are 12,595 persons in all, 6,918 being males and 5,677 females. There are thus 820.61 females per 1,000 males in the rural population. But while the population is not large we have to bear in mind that a number of people in the rural parts of Nahan tehsil are outsiders who come from other places to earn their living. They either take to hewing wood and supplying fuel to the town, or bringing grass, vegetables, and other necessaries or engagé as labourers in cultivation. Most of them do not bring their womenfolk and so an artificial disparity in the numbers of the sexes has been maintained. The other three tehsils, Paonta, Renka, and Pachhad, are inhabited by people who practise polyandry. But it is only in the trans-Giri parts of these tehsils that we come across

Year	Total (sq. miles)	Culti-vated (sq. miles)	Culti-vable but not culti-vated (sq. miles)	Under crops— 8-year average matur-ed (sq. miles)	Total Population			Urban Population			Rural Population		
					Total	Males	Females	Total	Males	Females	Total	Males	Females
1881	1,108	136	110	——	1,12,317	63,305	49,066	5,253	3,065	2,188	1,07,118	60,240	46,878
1891	1,108	140	100	——	1,24,134	69,268	54,866	6,121	3,643	2,478	1,18,013	65,625	52,388
1901	1,108	145	82	——	1,35,687	75,461	60,226	6,256	3,611	2,645	1,29,431	71,850	57,581
1911	1,108	151	77	——	1,38,520	76,044	62,476	6,341	3,636	2,705	1,32,179	72,408	59,771
1921	1,108	151	77	——	1,40,448	77,003	63,445	6,638	3,821	2,817	1,33,810	77,182	60,628
1931	1,141	150	147	228	1,48,568	82,384	66,184	7,808	4,584	3,224	1,40,760	77,800	62,960
Tehsils for 1931													
Nahan	186	14	9	20	20,403	11,502	8,901	7,808	4,584	3,224	12,595	6,918	5,677
Paunta	259	48	11	66	35,647	20,148	15,499	—	—	—	35,647	20,148	15,499
Renka	380	51	55	84	60,270	33,681	26,589	—	—	—	60,270	33,681	26,589
Pachhad	316	37	72	58	32,248	17 053	15,195	—	—	—	32,240	17,053	15,195

polyandry and only rarely in the cis-Giri parts of Renka tehsil. About a quarter of Pachhad tehsil does not now practise polyandry and it is only in the parts adjoining Renka tehsil where polyandry is found. We may now calculate the percentage of females for these tehsils:

	Total population	Males	Females	Females per 1,000 males
Nahan	20,403	11,502	8,901	773.86
Paonta	35,647	26,148	15,499	769.25
Renka	60,270	33,681	26,589	788.65
Pachhad	32,248	17,053	15,195	891.94

We had the following figures for Bikrami 1938 (1881 A.D.)

Nahan	*Paonta*	*Renka*	*Pachhad*
714.4	169.4	685.05	688.4

We may thus note the difference in the proportion of the sexes in 1881 and 1931

	Females per 1,000 males				
	Nahan	*Paonta*	*Renka*	*Pachhad*	*Total*
1881	714.4	169.4	685.05	688.4	775.07
1931	773.86	769.25	788.65	891.04	797.53

We find that there has been a marked difference in the proportion of the sexes between 1881 and 1931. While Renka has kept the steadiest pace Pachhad and Paonta have shown a remarkable increase in the number of females. Renka had 685.65 females per 1,000 males in 1931. Though there has been a rise in the number of females it is not extraordinary. The case of Nahan is not very different. It has shown an increase in the number of females from 714.4 per 1,000 in 1881 to 773.86 in 1931 for the simple reason that the urban population settled here with their women and children and so the artificial disparity has, to some extent, been lessened. But since a good deal of people still have a temporary abode here some disparity is natural. Polyandry is not practised in this tehsil. The number in Paonta and Pachhad went up from 169.4 and 688.4 females per 1,000 males in 1881 to 769.25 and 891.04 females per 1,000 males in 1931. This may call for some explanation. As we said earlier while discussing the *Sirmur Settlement Report* (1938) Bikrami (1881 A.D.), the part of Paonta tehsil which goes by the name of Doon was uninhabited in 1881. This part is considered to be most productive and fertile. It was unpopulated in 1881 and people from outside were invited to settle here. Sikhs, Bahtis, Labanas, Kahars and Jats, and Muslims migrated into the cis-Giri tract of this tehsil. These castes are all non-polyandrous. The population thus grew up from 8,697 in 1881 to 20,148 in 1931. Since these people settled there with their families the number of females for the tehsil greatly increased and we find that instead of having 169.4 females per 1,000 males as in 1881 it had 769.25 females in 1931. Thus the increase in the number of females in Paonta has occurred not because the people of the tehsil have in any appreciable number given up the practice of polyandry but because the most populous part of the tehsil has been inhabited by castes and tribes which do not follow polyandry and also because a predominantly polyandrous part of the tehsil, i.e. Kangra, was taken out of it and added to Renka. As far as the trans-Giri people of this tehsil are concerned, there has been no marked change in their customs or practices though polyandry does not possess exactly the same influence which it once had and it is sheer necessity which is still keeping it alive. A set of different circumstances has changed the proportion of the sexes in Pachhad tehsil where the number of females per 1,000 males has risen from 688.4 in 1881 to 891.04 in 1931. Due to its contact with the then neighbouring British district of Simla and the influence of modern ideas polyandry is found least in this trans-Giri tract of Sirmur. The markets of Simla, Kasauli, Dagshai, and Solan were accessible to the residents of Pachhad. The land was thus put to its maximum use and vegetables were supplied to these markets. Intensive cultivation became possible and the outlook of the people changed considerably. The areas of this tehsil near the polyandrous trans-Giri tract of Renka are, however, affected and show a greater disparity in the proportion of sexes. Polyandry was very common in Pachhad in 1881 but has lost very much of its hold on the people and even the trans-Giri tract of this tehsil is only moderately polyandrous. It is the most advanced tehsil in culture and civilization and has consequently been most progressive in eschewing undesirable practices and customs and adopting desirable ones.

Renka tehsil, situated in the inner recesses of the Himalayas and far removed from the approach of civilization, has been least affected and thus it has shown an increase from 685.05 females per 1,000 males in 1881 to only 788.65 per 1,000 males in 1931. It is the most backward tehsil and is the least subject to change. Though the influence of polyandry has been challenged even in this tehsil, it still holds its own especially in the interior such as Kangra and it will be some time before it is completely ousted from this area. It is only in the trans-Giri tracts of Pachhad, Paonta, and Renka that we find the people practising polyandry while the cis-Giri population of these tehsils is free from it. For a proper understanding of the position we have to find out the number of people residing in the trans-Giri tracts of these tehsils and if possible the proportion of the sexes. We have prepared the following chart for the trans-Giri people on the basis of the returns from the *Census of India* (1931). The following figures concern the trans-Giri tracts only and those for the cis-Giri tracts have been excluded.

Tehsil	Total	Males	Females	Females per 1,000 males
Pachhad	17,377	9,061	8,316	916.78
Paonta	15,241	8,623	6,618	767.47
Renka	55,398	31,109	24,289	780.77
Total	88,016	48,793	39,223	804.27

We get the following figures showing the difference between

the trans-Giri population and the total population of these tehsils for 1931:

Tehsil	Total	Males	Females	Females per 1,000 males
Pachhad	32,248	17,053	15,195	891.04
Trans-Giri tract of Pachhad	17,377	9,061	8,316	916.78
Paonta	35,647	20,148	15,499	769.25
Trans-Giri tract of Paonta	15,241	8,623	6,618	767.47
Renka	60,270	33,681	26,589	788.65
Trans-Giri tract of Renka	55,398	31,109	24,289	780.77

We notice that a greater part of the population of these tehsils resides in the trans-Giri territory except in the case of Paonta and the actual number of females per 1,000 males in the territory is less than what had been shown for the state except in the case of Pachhad. In the case of Paonta we find that there are in fact only 767.47 females per 1,000 males and not 769.25; in Renka only 780.77 females, per 1,000 males, and not 788.65 as shown for the whole tehsil. Pachhad, as we stated before, stands on a different footing in as much as the people of this tehsil have practically given up polyandry and economic and sociological factors have come to the front which have resulted in an increase in the number of females. But when we consider that Pachhad has practically done away with polyandry our table showing 916.78 females per 1,000 males explains itself. We collected figures to indicate the actual number of males and females in the polyandrous tracts and in those areas which lie near them. We have collected figures for the trans-Giri villages on the boundary of Renka and Pachhad, for the trans-Giri villages in the polyandrous tract of Renka, for the villages in the non-polyandrous trans-Giri and cis-Giri villages of Pachhad, and the trans-Giri polyandrous villages of Paonta. The picture which emerges from the study of the sex-ratio in 70 polyandrous villages of Renka tehsil, 42 polyandrous villages of Paonta tehsil, 33 villages on the boundary of Renka and Pachhad in Renka tehsil, 12 villages in Pachhad tehsil, 18 non-polyandrous villages of trans-Giri, and 16 and 12 non-polyandrous villages of Pachhad and Paonta respectively is as follows:

	Name of area	Number of villages studied	Males	Females	Total	Females per 1,000 males
1.	Trans-Giri polyandrous tract of Renka tehsil	70	16,130	11,539	37,669	714.13
2.	Trans-Giri polyandrous tract of Paonta tehsil	42	7,136	5,547	12,683	763.31
3.	Trans-Giri villages on the boundary of Renka and Pachhad in Renka tehsil	33	2,630	2,397	5,027	911.4
4.	Trans-Giri villages on the boundary of Renka and Pachhad in Pachhad tehsil	12	1,034	970	2,004	938.1
5.	Non-polyandrous trans-Giri tract of Pachhad	18	1,183	1,178	2,361	995.77
6.	Cis-Giri non-polyandrous tract of Pachhad	16	1,110	1,149	2,259	1,035.13
7.	Cis-Giri non-polyandrous tract in Paonta	12	1,098	967	2,065	880.69

Except for serial numbers 6 and 7 the above table refers to the trans-Giri tract and figures for the cis-Giri tract are taken to show the contrast in the proportion of the sexes between localities where polyandry is practised and those where it is not. The greatest disparity in the proportion of the sexes is to be noticed in the polyandrous tracts of Renka and Paonta where we find only 714.13 and 763.31 females per 1,000 males. The disparity is specially noticeable in the case of Renka tehsil because we collected figures for this area chiefly from Kangra and its surroundings, the most polyandrous part of the state. The percentage for whole trans-Giri area of Renka tehsil comes to 780.77 females per 1,000 males naturally because it includes tracts where the practice is dying out, e.g. near the cis-Giri and Pachhad. But the practice has been least effected in Kangra and thus the figures fall to 714.13 females per 1,000 males for that area. Pachhad has practically given up polyandry though a few persons may still find it convenient or necessary to share common wives. But the figures given in table on page 124 show the marked difference in the proportion of the sexes in villages which are on the boundaries of the two tehsils. While in villages near the boundary line of Renka tehsil there are 911.4 females per 1,000 males, in Pachhad tehsil near the boundary line we find 938.1 females per 1,000 males. In other parts of the trans-Giri tract where polyandry is not practised there are 995.77 females per 1,000 males and in the non-polyandrous cis-Giri tract of Pachhad we find as many as 1035.13 females per 1,000 males. We may conclude from these figures that the disparity in the proportion of the sexes is most marked in the polyandrous trans-Giri tract of Renka. It is less marked in villages in the same tehsil which are on the boundary line between Renka and Pachhad tehsils, and still less in villages in Pachhad tehsil on the boundary of these two tehsils, and still less in the non-polyandrous trans-Giri tract of Pachhad and turns the other way round in the case of the cis-Giri non-polyandrous tract of Pachhad. In areas where polyandry is not practised we find that the number of the males and females tends to be equal and it is only in areas where polyandry is practised that any great divergence in the numbers of the sexes is noticeable. The proportional increase in the number of females in the cis-Giri non-polyandrous tract of Pachhad may be due to the practice of polygyny which is commonly resorted

to by all those who can afford it. We notice the same phenomenon working in Paonta tehsil. In the polyandrous tract of
Paonta which lies in trans-Giri there are 763.31 females per
1,000 males but in the non-polyandrous cis-Giri tract there are
880.69 females per 1,000 males. There were a number of villages on the other side of the Giri, not mentioned in the tables,
which had quite a marked difference between the number of
males and females; as in the case of Chandni in Paonta which
had 79 males and 49 females. We should have taken the number
of males and females on both sides of the Giri in Paonta tehsil as
we have done in the case of Pacnhad but the trans-Giri area of
Paonta tehsil is very small and does not give scope for a useful
collection of figures on that basis. We have, therefore, confined
ourselves to the collection of figures for the polyandrous trans-
Giri tract in Paonta and for the non-polyandrous cis-Giri tract
in the same area.

It is clear from the figures given above that the greatest
disparity in the proportion of the sexes is to be noticed in the
trans-Giri tracts of Renka and Paonta tehsils and that it is in
these areas that polyandry still holds its own due to a great
extent to the scarcity of women. In areas where there is no
such scarcity and men can easily find mates polyandry does
not find a suitable soil and is not practised to any appreciable
extent. But it is bound to affect a people among whom women
are scarce and men cannot find separate mates for themselves.
If we consider the fact that the inhabitants of the trans-Giri
tract in Renka tehsil have only 714.13 females per 1,000 males
we may appreciate the difficulty of the males in finding separate
wives for themselves. In a community where out of 1,000
males there are roughly 300 males who cannot in any case find
mates for themselves the matter of getting wives not only to
satisfy their natural desires but to manage their household
would present a serious problem to the men. Other considerations also, such as scarcity of land and the insecurity of a tract
where women cannot be left alone for any length of time, may
have led to the introduction of the practice of polyandry in
this and other regions. Scarcity of women has polyandry as its
sequel. One interesting fact which these people brought to our

notice was that, besides preventing excessible sub-division of holdings and limiting the increase of population, polyandry also resulted in the procreation of more male children who were better suited to stand the rigours of life here. At first sight both these advantages may seem remote and unimportant. But on a closer examination one may not fail to see the validity and strength of these results as arguments for polyandry. Where two, three, or more brothers have a joint wife they are likely to procreate fewer children than if every one of them had a wife exclusively for himself. We may assume that on an average there are four brothers for one joint wife in the polyandrous trans-Giri tract. They can have at most one child in a year but if all four of them had separate wives they might have as many as four children in a year or at least two or three. We have considered only one family consisting of four brothers and a wife and have noted that in such a case the birth of children has been greatly checked and the family has not increased as it naturally would have done otherwise. Thus in a country whose resources cannot cope with a numerous population polyandry offers an easy solution by checking the natural increase. Further, it probably results in the procreation of more boys than girls. The following table based on the study of families in the trans-Giri polyandrous tract of Renka tehsil corroborates this view :

Names of husbands	Caste	Name of village	Name of wife	Total number of births	Male births	Female births
I (i) Dhyanoo (ii) Chandnoo (iii) Jheroo (iv) Shiboo (v) H ra (vi) Jhinjiyaroo	Kanet	Rajana	Pashlo	2	1	1
II (i) Mainsingh (ii) Budh Ram (iii) Bali Ram (iv) Kanshi Ram	Kanet	Kundar	Kinkri	2	2	—

III	(i) Kanthi Ram	Kanet	Kundar	Shaoni	3	1	2 One girl is dead
	(ii) Mina						
IV	(i) Dhanda	Koli	Kundar	Bholloo	4	3	1
	(ii) Chanota						
	(iii) Dholoo						
	(iv) Nahntoo						
V	(i) Khayoo	Koli	Kundar	Laboo	13	11	2
	(ii) Toploo						
VI	(i) Andhoa	Koli	Kundar	Janko	5	3	2
	(ii) Munia						
	(iii) Ladar						
VII	(i) Shaonoo	Kanet	Rajana	Ramsi	5	5	—
	(ii) Jundha						
	(iii) Noora						
	(iv) Nahntoo						
	(v) Bali						
VIII	(i) Bhatkoo	Kanet	Rajana	Kalmi	2	2	—
	(ii) Kevta						
	(iii) Dhelroo						
IX	(i) Mojee	Bhat	Rajana	Bholoo	6	3	3
	(ii) Choonchoo						
X	(i) Devisingh	Bhat	Kolath	Sundri	7	4	3
	(ii) Sobha Ram						
XI	(i) Devi Ram	Bhat	Kolath	Gonesho	5	4	1
	(ii) Mohi Ram						
XII	(i) Phagoo	Bhat	Kolath	Sadhti	6	5	1
	(ii) Tulsi Ram						
XIII	(i) Bhookia	Kanet	Rajana	Runon	3	1	2
	(ii) Devisingh						
XIV	(i) Devi Ram	Bhat	Rajana	Kalo	2	2	—
	(ii) Sobha						
	(iii) Kalia						
XV	(i) Dheliya	Kanet	Rajana	Bhori	2	1	1
	(ii) Kalia Ram						
XVI	(i) Dharam Singh	Kanet	Rajana	Negti	5	4	1 The girl is dead
	(ii) Sobha						
	(iii) Devi Singh						
XVII	(i) Ram Nath	Bhat	Baonal	Minke	6	5	1
	(ii) Tulia						
	(iii) Budhia.						
XVIII	(i) Khyali Ram	Bhat	Baonal	Sanki	3	2	1

	(ii) Chuhia						
	(iii) Mina						
XIX	(i) Dhirjoo	Koli	Bag	Nakti	7	5	2
	(ii) Mali						
XX	(i) Dholoo						
	(ii) Kiaroo	Koli	Baonal	Pashlo	2	2	1
XXI	(i) Bhoora						
	(ii) Jhakloo	Koli	Bag	Ganesho	9	5	4
							Two girls are dead
					99	71	28

The same indications are to be found in Table VII (Age, Sex and Civil condition) of the *Census of India* (Punjab, Sirmur State) regarding the number of persons between the age of 0-1.

Total	*Males*	*Females*
3,551	1,830	1,721

These are figures for the whole of the state but in the trans-Giri tract, especially the polyandrous area, we find that the disparity between the numbers of male and female births is still more marked and more male children are born than female. If that were not so the disparity we have in the proportion of the sexes would not have been possible.

The custom of polyandry is defended by those who practise it on the ground that it prevents both economic pressure due to increase of family and subdivision of property in a country where agricultural land is not sufficient for the needs of its inhabitants. The total area of Bashahr state was 3,820 square miles while the population in 1901 was 80,572. No statistics are unfortunately available of the cultivable, cultivated, and uncultivable areas of the state. But it is a fact that a greater part of the state consists of high mountains and precipitous rocks where no cultivation is possible. Agriculture is confined to a limited area and is not enough to support the cultivators. They have, therefore, to take to sheep, goat, and pony-breeding as supplementary occupations and a number of persons have to keep away from home most of the time. Polyandry enables a family of brothers to get the full benefit of several sources of livelihood. One can cultivate the joint land, another breed cattle, a third engage in trade, and so on. General Cunningham, writing about Ladakh in this connection, strongly supports this custom. He says that polyandry is the principal check to the increase of population and, however revolting it may be to our feelings, it was a most politic measure for a poor country which does not produce sufficient food for its inhabitants.

Polyandry was in former times directly encouraged by the state which imposed penalty on partitions.[1] If the brothers divided moveable property one half share of the whole was taken over by the state and divisions of immovable property were refused official recognition. This fact goes a long way to prove that the state government was decidedly of the opinion that the country could not afford partitions and fragmentations of holdings as there was very little cultivable land available. What little was available would be made useless by splitting it up into uneconomic and insignificantly small plots and the state would not be in a position even to realize its revenue.

Polyandry is not practised in the Kangra district proper but it is practised in Kullu, Saraj, and Lahaul. It is common throughout Saraj, and in parts of Waziri Rupee as also in the isolated Molana glen in the Kullu region. Of these localities the most congested in population is Kullu proper. The grain produced there is insufficient to afford food to the people and a certain amount of corn has to be imported every year. According to the *Kangra District Gazetteer* (1924-25), Kangra had an area of 2,544 and Kullu 1,335 square miles. The total area thus comes to 3,879 square miles. The population was 3,13,277. Out of 2,544 square miles in Kangra only 769 square miles were cultivated so that the pressure on the cultivated area was 837 persons to a square mile. The provincial density was only 217 persons per square mile (in Kangra it was 281) and the density on the cultivated area was, according to 1911 figures, 499 persons per square mile. But it was

[1]*Punjab States Gazetteer*, Vol. VII, Simla Hill States, 1910, Bashahr State, Part A, p. 16.

only in Kullu, Saraj. and Lahaul that polyandry was found. The tables on pages 132-33 show the conditions in Kullu and Saraj. It will be clear from these tables how congested Kullu and Saraj are and how cultivation is difficult in those areas. The highest density of population is of course seen in Kangra and Palampur. But we have to bear in mind that Kangra is in a much better position than any other locality in the district. Palampur comes next. Kangra tehsil possesses a town and is naturally in a better position to support its people. They can easily transport their produce to the market at Kangra and are otherwise in a better position to attend to their lands. Out of a total area of 429 and 443 square miles for Kangra and Palampur respectively they have cultivated areas of 99 and 125 square miles respectively or 23 per cent and 28.2 per cent of the total area is under cultivation. In the case of Kullu and Saraj, however, we find that out of an area of 1,342 square miles only 125 square miles is under cultivation. In other words, only 9.3 per cent of the total area is under cultivation. Though apparently Kangra and Palampur have a greater density of population than Kullu and Saraj, in fact Kullu and Saraj have reached the maximum to which the land could carry them and only 9.2 per cent of the total area has practically the same density as 23 per cent and 28 per cent of the total areas in Kangra and Palampur. One other important factor which has to be noted in this connection is that while in Kangra and Palampur there are still 40 and 53 square miles respectively of land which could be brought under cultivation, Kullu and Saraj have practically exhausted all cultivable lands and only 12 and 13 square miles of cultivable land respectively may still be brought under cultivation. The density in other parts of the district, such as Nurpur, Dehra, and Hamirpur, is only 666.9, 766.8, and 715.4 per square mile respectively as compared with 998.4 per square mile of Kullu and Saraj. These tracts have 75, 124, and 102 square miles of land respectively still left uncultivated though they can be brought under cultivation. The inhabitants of Kullu and Saraj, therefore, having exhausted the land and not having the prospect of any more cultivable land, have had to devise means for providing for themselves and thus very probably had recourse to polyandry. For this

Tehsil	Total (sq. miles)	Cultivated (sq. miles)	Cultivable but not cultivated (sq. miles)	Under matured crops, 10 years' average (sq. miles)	Total population			Urban population			Rural population			Density per sq. mile of cultivated area (rural)
					Total	Males	Females	Total	Males	Females	Total	Males	Females	
District (1911)	9,574	912	419	1,022	770,38	401,109	369,277	6,923	4,795	2,128	763,463	396,314	367,149	837.1
Kangra	429	99	40	143	119,628	64,168	55,460	6,923	4,795	2,128	112,705	59,378	53,332	1138.4
Palampur	443	125	53	180	132,688	67,825	64,863	—	—	—	132,688	67,825	64,863	1061.1
Nurpur	525	165	75	142	100,041	56,494	43,547	—	—	—	100,041	56,494	43,547	666.9
Hamirpur	601	233	102	240	166,701	84,892	81,809	—	—	—	166,701	84,892	81,809	715.4
Dehra	516	165	124	169	12,625	65,608	60,917	—	—	—	12,625	65,608	60,917	766.8
Kulu	1,054	67	12	83 }										
Saraj	288	58	13	65 }	124,803	62,122	62,681	—	—	—	124,803	62,122	62,681	998.4

SURVERY AND ASSESSED AREA FOR DISTRICT AND TEHSILS

Tehsil	Year	Total area including forest	Total area available for cultivation not yet cultivated		Total cultivated area	Total assessment (in rupees)
			Government waste	Other		
Kulu	1893	6,93,618	3,869	6,945	42,742	69,307
	1901-1902	6,74,387	6,16,370	7,615	42,629	69,804
	1906-1907	62,291	—	8,114	42,272	69,851
	1910-1911	62,329	31	7,559	42,989	69,853
Saraj	1893	1,84,306	3,160	8,648	35,756	38,840
	1901-1902	1,84,617	3,122	8,417	36,467	38,840
	1906-1907	1,84,751	—	8,584	36,341	38,839
	1910-1911	1,83,431	—	7,904	36,874	38,839

total cultivated area of 125 square miles together with the waste lands they had to pay Rs 108,690 a year. Naturally they found refuse in a custom which allowed them to live on communal lines and, by sharing all the assets and liabilities, to eke out a meagre and bare living in such adverse circumstances. There was no scope either for extending cultivation, or partitioning land or indulging in the luxury of having a separate wife. The cost of individually maintaining a wife and a separate household was too great to foster monogamous families and the people looked on the custom without disfavour.

Land in these Himalayan tracts has been put to its maximum use and every inch of space fit for cultivation has been brought under the plough. We find that though Simla has only an average density of 209 of rural population per square mile, the average density per square mile of sown area is 664 for 1931. Simla, of course, has the advantage of being in a position in which the people can take to producing vegetables and selling milk and have also a field for employments of varied kinds. But apart from Simla one notices that every available piece of land in the country has been brought under cultivation and people earn their living by subsidiary industries such as bee-keeping, sheepbreeding, weaving, and the like. Vast tracts of land lie barren and the whole pressure of the population is thrown on those pieces of land which are available for cultivation and every small field has to support a number of members of a family. Partitions are not possible and the only way to stop the subdivision of holdings is for each person to merge his individuality in the group and manage everything on the fraternal basis. A visit to Jubbal and other hill states in the interior would have convinced one of the utter helplessness of their people and how the land was finding it hard to maintain the population.

The total population of Jubbal in 1901 was 21,172. The density of population in the state in 1931, if the whole area be taken, is 74.03 per square mile. According to the revenue returns (1901), the total area of the state is 1,82,124 acres, 10 per cent of which is cultivated, 36 per cent under forest, and 54 per cent is uncultivated waste land. Out of the latter 25 per cent is *ghasni* (grazing land). The total area of the state is 284.5 square miles. Out of this area only 10 per cent is under cultivation and 90 per cent is either forest or waste land. In other words only 28.45 square miles is under cultivation. It is natural that in such a country, where only 10 per cent of land is under cultivation and the rest is all forest or waste land, the people would feel the necessity of exploiting the land to its utmost capacity and of avoiding that division of holdings which would deprive them of even a bare living. Coupled with that is the scarcity of females and the interaction of these two factors, together with the extreme poverty of the people, seems to provide ideal conditions for the working of polyandry in these hills.

We shall, therefore, at the outset find out the density of population in the areas with which we are concerned. We may start with the figures given on pages 136-37 for 1931 from *Sirmur State Gazetteer*. In order to find out the actual pressure of population on a hilly country, such as Simla hill states and Sirmur, one has to consider the pressure of population on the cultivated area and compare it with that of other states, districts, or countries which are more prosperous to form an idea whether any further sub-divisions of land are feasible or not in such an area. It is clear that the density of 130 per square mile for Sirmur is not heavy for many countries in the West have a density much higher than this. But a consideration of the actual state of things will convince us of the great pressure to which land in this area has been subjected and how no further partitions or subdivisions are economically possible. On referring to the table of Sirmur state (on page 137) we notice that Pachhad tehsil has a density of 102, Nahan of 109, Paonta of 137, and Renka of 158 per square mile. Paonta and Nahan have more level lands and polyandry is not practised in Nahan and the cis-Giri tract of Paonta. Though the trans-Giri area of Pachhad is hilly the cis-Giri area is not predominantly so and a considerable portion of it can be brought under the plough although malaria and the veneral diseases have resulted in turning some of these lands into wastes so that a low density of population is discernible here. Renka tehsil, on the other hand, cut off from

Tehsils	Total (sq. miles)	Cultivated (sq. miles)	Cultivable but not cultivated (sq. miles)	Under crops 8-year average (sq. miles)	Total population			Urban population			Rural population		
					Total	Males	Females	Total	Males	Females	Total	Males	Females
Nahan	186	14	9	20	20,403	11,502	8,901	7,808	4,584	3,224	12,595	6,918	5,677
Paonta	259	48	11	66	35,647	20,148	15,499	—	—	—	35,647	20,148	15,499
Renka	380	51	55	84	60,270	33,681	26,581	—	—	—	60,270	33,681	26,589
Pachhad	316	37	72	58	32,248	17,053	15,195	—	—	—	32,248	17,053	15,195

On the basis of the above table we arrive at the following figures :

Tehsil	Total (sq. miles)	Cultivated (sq. miles)	Cultivable but not cultivated (sq. miles)	Total population	Population on cultivated land per sq. mile	Cultivated land in kacha bighas	Distribution of population per 100 kacha bighas	Population in town
Nahan	186	14	9	20,403	899.6	44,435	28.3	7,808
Paonta	259	48	11	35,647	742.6	1,49,695	23.7	
Renka	380	51	55	60,270	1,181.7	1,56,651	38.4	
Pachhad	316	37	72	32,248	871.5	1,15,368	27.9	

DENSITY PER SQUARE MILE

Tehsil	Total (sq. miles)	Total population	Density per sq. mile	Average density per sq. mile
Nahan	186	20,503 (rural 12,595)	109.6	
				130.2
Paonta	259	35,647	137.5	
Renka	380	60,270	158.6	
Pachhad	316	32,248	102.0	

civilization, handicapped by the most unfavourable physical surroundings, having barren uninhabitable and uncultivable mountains where there is complete lack of conveyance, has the greatest density per square mile, e.g. 158. But we have to see what the actual pressure of population is by leaving out the unproductive portion of the area. It is apparent that about 10 per cent of the total area bears this burden on land and as much as 90 per cent, as in the case of Jubbal, remains waste. The table on page 138 for survey and assessed area (in *kachha bighas*) for the whole state of Sirmur may be useful.

We find that only 13 per cent of the total land is under cultivation. Out of 3,550,081 *kachha bighas* of land only 466,949 is under cultivation, 36,123 is government waste, and 2,600,176 is uncultivable including forests. Thus 2,636,299 kachha bighas of land out of a total area of 3,550,081 is uncultivable. In other words, 74 per cent of the total can be brought under the plough. But even that may be found to be unfit for cultivation. The area under cultivation in fact bears the total pressure of population. Even then we have to note that those tracts which have comparatively wide, open, and level fields have greater areas of uncultivated land than those, like Renka and Pachhad, which have a much greater number of precipitous hills and uncultivable pieces of land. In the case of Nahan and Paonta, many tracts which could be brought under cultivation are lying waste but this can hardly be said of Pachhad and especially of Renka where every possible plot has been brought under plough.

State or Tehsil	Year	Total area including forests	Government waste	Total area available for cultivation but not yet cultivated	Total cultivated area	Total assessment including that of Muafis and Jagirs	Area uncultivable including forests	Percentage of cultivated land in total area of the State
Sirmur State	1933-34	3,550,081	36,123	447,623	466,949	311,028	2,600,176	13.1
Tehsils								
Nahan	,,	574,594	1,844	26,318	44,435	24,560	501,997	7.7
Paonta	,,	837,299	6,032	33,311	149,695	68,063	648,261	17.8
Renka	,,	1,166,171	15,813	166,310	156,651	117,118	823,397	13.6
Pachhad	,,	972,017	12,434	221,684	115,368	101,287	622,531	11.8

The following table shows the state of cultivation:

Tehsil	Total area including forests	Government waste	Area cultivable but not cultivated	Cultivated area	Uncultivated area	Percentage of cultivated total area
Nahan	574,594	1,844	26,318	44,435	501,997	7.7
Paonta	837,299	6,032	33,311	149,695	648,261	17.8
Renka	1,166,171	15,813	166,310	156,651	117,118	13.6
Pachhad	972,017	12,434	221,684	115,368	101,287	11.8

Tehsil	Total sq. miles	Culti-vated sq. miles	Sq. miles cultiva-ble but not culti-vated	Total popul-ation	Population on cultiva-ted land per sq. mile	Cultivated land in kachha bighas	Distribution of population per 100 kachha bighas
Nahan	186	14	9	20,403	899.6	44,435	28.3
Paonta	259	48	11	35,647	742.6	149,695	23.7
Renka	380	51	55	60,270	1,181.7	156.651	38.4
Pachhad	316	37	72	32,248	871,5	115,368	27.9

One kachha bigha is equal to 5/24 acre and one acre is equal
to 4,840 square yards. In order to realize the implications
of the pressure of population on the land we may have to
consider the pressure on cultivated land and then see how it
compares with that of other places. The table on page 139
concerning Sirmur state may elucidate the point.

We thus find that the four tehsils of Sirmur have the following density per square mile:

Nahan	899.6
Paonta	742.6
Renka	1,181.7
Pachhad	871.5

For the sake of comparison we may give the incidence of
the rural population per square mile in 1931 on the matured
area for the other districts of the region and Sirmur state.

District of the region	Population per square mile on the matured area	Sirmur state	Population per square mile on the matured area
Kangra	804	Renka	1,181.7
Hoshiarpur	789	Nahan	899.6
Simla	733	Pachhad	871.3
Sialkot	681	Paonta	742.6

While the most densely populated rural district of Kangra
has a density of 804 persons on the matured area, the most
densely populated tehsil, the polyandrous tehsil of Sirmur state,
has a density of 1,181 persons per square mile. Renka tehsil
thus supports 377 persons per square mile, more than the
most favoured and densely populated district of Kangra. The
other tehsils follow closely behind. Nahan has a density of
899 persons per square mile and even Pachhad has a density of
871.5. Paonta tehsil, though hilly and unapproachable as far
as its trans-Giri-polyandrous tract is concerned, has, with its
wide, open and fertile fields in the cis-Giri, only a density of
742.6 which compares favourably with the best and most densely populated districts of Punjab. We have to consider the
cause of this great density of population in such an out of the
way place. There certainly is one advantage which this state
and all other tracts of the Himalayas have and that is copious
rainfall. Since the tract is hilly abundance of rainfall and water

is natural. Whatever other drawbacks the hills may have they always have a good rainfall. The plain portion of Paonta, called the Doon, has some other advantages which the other parts of the state do not have. It is mostly level and its produce can easily be carried to market by the producer. The residents of Nahan tehsil too are favourably placed. The capital of the state is situated in this tehsil and affords ample opportunity to the people to have all sorts of employment and to supply vegetables, milk, etc., to the town. They can bring all their produce to Nahan or send them on to Sadhaura or Ambala with which it is connected by a good road. But the condition of the hilly tracts, especially the trans-Giri, is peculiar. The people there live under particularly unfavourable circumstances. It is the hard labour of the people which maintains them on the soil in this tract and in that men, women, and even children play their due part. Apart from agriculture, Simla, Dagshai, Mussourie, and Chakrata afford the residents of this locality some scope to earn their living as manual labourers. In the cold weather, when all other activities are suspended because of the snow, and even in summer, a member or more per family, from those villages which are more adventurous than the rest, move to these towns and after serving there for some time return home. In this way they manage to add a little to their family income and pay the land revenue and the dues of the village Sahukar or other moneylenders. Except for this temporary absence, the average agriculturist stays at home and attends to his lands and cattle. He has to depend mainly on his land and only the matured area yields him any produce and the family works hard on it.

Women work hardest on the land. As is evident, the land is supporting the maximum number of people. The land of Renka tehsil, cut off from civilization and devoid of marketing and other facilities, has a density of 1,181 persons per square mile of matured area. The people do not want to move out and stick to the land whatever may happen. The only possible way in which this can continue is by keeping the members of a family together and not allow any sub-division. As the table (see p. 139) shows, Renka tehsil has a distribution of 38 persons per 100 kachcha bighas of land which means that one person cannot have even three kachcha bighas of land of the matured area for cultivation and cannot earn his living from it. If there are partitions the land would be so sub-divided that it would leave worthless fragments for cultivation which could not maintain a family. In Renka tehsil only 13 per cent of the land is cultivated and few realize under what difficult conditions cultivation is carried on there. The total area of the tehsil is 380 square miles and only 51 square miles is under cultivation, 55 square miles are entered as cultivable but not cultivated. As a matter of fact, the real figure would be much less because all the land regarded as cultivable can never be brought under cultivation and all possibly cultivable land has already been brought under the plough. But even if it be granted that all that land could be cultivated, we are left only with 55 square miles of land in Renka tehsil, 11 in Paonta, nine in Nahan, and 72 in Pachchad. If all these lands could be cultivated they could not have sustained the increase of population which would have resulted if the institution of polyandry had not been introduced in those tracts. The land fit for cultivation is so little that, in a short space of time, sub-division and fragmentation of holdings would have reduced the whole of it into a useless tract which could not even supply enough food to its owners. But before this could happen the society devised means for avoiding sub-division and fragmentation of holdings and kept the family intact by wedding the brothers to one common wife and thus checking both the growth of population and division in the family. The assumption, therefore, that the cause of polyandary lies in the desire to transmit an estate undivided gains added proof from the study of local agriculture. If land were ample and there were scope for expansion of cultivation this custom could hardly continue in the teeth of the opposition it has to face and the feeling of inferiority it produces. But a visit to the country convinces one that hardly any expansion of cultivation is possible and strenuous efforts have been made by the people to bring every inch of land under cultivation.

They are anxious to acquire more land and are prepared to pay a heavy price for it. Land is, therefore, dearest in the trans-

Giri tract. While land is available in the non-polyandrous cis-Giri tract of Pachhad tehsil, there is no room for expansion of cultivation in the trans-Giri, especially in Renka. But it is not only in the trans-Giri tract of Renka that this scarcity of land and the desire to transmit an estate undivided exists side by side with polyandry but in the whole of the Himalayan region where this practice prevails the same conditions are found working. Whether we consider the residents of Lahul or Chamba Lahul, or Kullu, Saraj and Kanaur, Jaunsar-Bawar or the trans-Giri polyandrous tract of Sirmur, we find that scarcity of land is common to all and has greatly influenced the continuance, if not the origin, of the institution of polyandry. How far the desire to keep an estate undivided after the death of an owner was responsible for it can be best judged from the case of Bashahr state where the administration actively encouraged it and imposed penalty on partitions. No better proof could be afforded of the influence of this factor. That was also most probably the reason why the Jathong and Kanchong systems of inheritance prevailed in these polyandrous tracts. Surprising as it may appear, the customs bore the same names in Bashahr, Sirmur, and other polyandrous parts of the hills. "Jathong" from "jetha" or elder means the right of the elder and "kanchong" from "kancha" or youngest means the right of the youngest brother. Since partitions were to be discouraged check was placed by society on them by enforcing the rights of the eldest and youngest brothers. If a partition has to take place a good field has to be given to the eldest brother according to jathong and the ancestral house has to be given to the youngest brother according to kanchong. The customs seem to imply the assumptions that the youngest brother is too young to find a new home for himself and the eldest is entitled to some recognition of his seniority. But while these assumptions may be far, what is more likely is that in addition to these, or probably as the origin of these, was the desire to levy some conditions which, though not obnoxious to the members of the family, might work as a suitable check on the desire to have partitions affected. After keeping apart a good field for the eldest and the ancestral house for the youngest, the rest of the property had to be divided equally among all the brothers. Thus in a family of six brothers, in case of partition, the eldest would get one good extra field and the youngest the ancestral house and the rest of the property would be equally divided among them all. While the eldest and the youngest are gainers, the other four brothers are the losers. They lose one good field and, what is more, the ancestral house. They must make one or more houses for themselves and spend their time, energy, and money on them, while they gain nothing by partition. It would therefore be to their interest not to burden themselves with this extra expenditure but to get what benefits they could from the family property as such. While, therefore, the eldest and the youngest may desire a partition, the majority of brothers would be against it and would try all they could to avoid it. Thus, while in an ordinary joint Hindu family all the brothers get equal shares in the family property, the polyandrous people of the hills laid these two conditions on the members of a family so that in case of partition the interests of the majority of brothers are generally against partition. Thus, in an indirect but effective manner, the desire to transmit an estate undivided was secured though apparently jathong and kanchong only safeguarded the interests of the eldest and the youngest brothers. Apart from these considerations the question of the allotment of the wife would prove a serious problem. On a partition she would go to the husband who had originally brought her in marriage and the other brothers would have to go without a wife. They may now get separate wives or may form a fresh *joridari* (joint family) and get another common wife but then they have again to pool their shares together and the woman and the property would remain joint. We have seen how difficult it is to get a wife in the hills, especially in the trans-Giri tract of Sirmur, and how the people can ill-afford to carry out partitions.

Another factor which has not been discussed so far is the peculiar circumstances in which the original inhabitants had to live in these hills. In a country where, in spite of the fact that cultivation has made great headway and the density of population has risen up to 1,181 per square mile, we find even today only 51 square miles of cultivated land out of 380, there

must have existed some other source of maintenance for the
people when they settled there. Agriculture alone could not
have yielded, as it cannot even now, sufficient means of
sustenance. The people had to find other ways and the two
most important of these, which still hold their own, were sheep
and goat-breeding. One of the brothers took charge of the
sheep and goats and went away to those places where there
were grazing grounds and other facilities. The sheep were a
necessity because in a cold place it is impossible to do without
warm clothing which the people could not afford to buy due to
their poverty. They had therefore to keep sheep and manufacture
their own woollen clothings. Sheep and cattle-rearing meant
that one member of the family had practically always to be
absent from home. If the family consisted only of a husband
and a wife this would present great difficulties for them. While
it would not be feasible for the husband to leave cultivation to
his wife alone, danger and difficulty would surround a woman left
to herself in her house during the prolonged absence of her husband. He may have to go with the sheep or cattle or he may
have to go to the dochhi and the wife would have to be left
alone. This could hardly be done in those days. She needed
someone to protect her in his absence. Polyandry, instead of
forming separate families, obtained a joint wife and avoided
all the difficulties which a separate wife for each would have
entailed. By keeping the brothers joint polyandry ensured a
division of labour and an efficiency which would not have been
possible otherwise and which alone have stood the rigours of
life here. As the morning dawns all the brothers are at their
respective posts. The one who has to stay at home attends to
the requirements there, the second goes to bring fuel, the third
to bring grass, the fourth with the sheep, the fifth to the
dochhi, and so on. Every one has enough work to do and none
sits idle like a peasant of the plains who has nothing to do for
most of the year. A hill is never free. He has work in every
season and every moment. Every one attends to the work
allotted to him and to avoid monotony there is constant change
of work. One who has remained absent for a long time receives
special consideration when he returns home. The housewife

attends to him exclusively and the other brothers do not grudge her special favours. When the husbands come home, after putting in a day's hard work, the joint wife offers them the hukkah, their favourite smoke, gives them water to bathe, and then serves them their meals. Everyone is attended to properly, impartially, and considerately and each feels happy at the end of the day. The working of the family on fraternal lines not only checks its disintegration but controls the increase of population and the division of property and results in efficiency of labour. Instead of lying idle for a part of the year or not having enough hands for the multifarious subsidiary occupations which life in the hills imposes, the joint undivided polyandrous family is able to utilize the time, energy, and services of every member of the family and maintains itself in the face of extremely hard and unfavourable circumstances. Division of labour and allocation of duties are never causes of disruption. If one brother works as a herdsman, another as a blacksmith, another as a labourer at Simla or some other place, and another on the field, the proceeds of their labour are pooled and each enjoys an equal part of the total income.

While polyandry in these hills has been found to be due to scarcity of women and land and a desire to leave an estate undivided, tradition has played no less significant role in sustaining the custom. The Pandava brothers had a common spouse and when her father raised an objection to the union of his daughter with five husbands, Yudhishthira told him on the authority of old practice that they had to take the path which their forefathers had followed.[3] Now this region is associated with the life and exploits of Arjuna who conquered it and indeed the people of the area are divided into two sections: Shathis and Pashis, after the Pandavas and Kauravas. Nor is polyandry instanced only by the Pandava brothers. It seems to have been a not unfamiliar custom in ancient India. Muni's daughter Varkshi had regular intercourse with ten

[3]*Mahabharata*, 1, 169.
[4]*Vishnu Purana*, 1 15, *Agni*, XVIII, *Bhagwata*, IV, 30-420.
[5]*Mahabharata*, 1, 209-212

Prasetas brothers.[4] The Daitya brothers, Sunda and Upasunda, held all three worlds under their rule of terror until the Apsara Trilottama, through her peerless loveliness, so strongly fascinated both of them that they slew each other.[5] Dhrishtadyumna protests against the younger brother's wife being shared by the elder but that the younger brothers should have access to the wife of the elder appears to him not at all unnatural or unlawful.[6] This corresponds with the arrangement in group marriage and is reflected in the mythical tale in the *Mahabharata* of the Rishi Utathya's younger brother Brihaspati who forced himself on Mamta, wife of the elder.[7] The Pandava tradition has determined the moral and social attitude of the people, lending them support in adhering to polyandry in spite of the gibes and reproaches of the monogamous people of the plains.

It should be noted that in 1881 A.D. there was certainly a very great disparity in the proportion of the sexes in Sirmur and in 1884 Thornton had noted that polyandry was universal in the state. Report, however, restricted it to those tracts of the trans-Giri where it is found even today. There is no evidence to show that polyandry of the pure form was ever practised in the whole state, especially in the cis-Giri. The customs and habits of the people do not present any data on the strength of which one could assume that it was universally practised among them in the past. It is of course true that the outlook of the people was communal or fraternal and not so individualistic as it is today. In those parts of the state where polyandry in the strict sense of the term was not practised, a woman had only one husband and she could acquire another only after securing divorce from him by paying him the Reet money or after his death. The brothers of the husband could, however, in his lifetime have sexual access to his wife. This may have been due to the working of the principle of fraternal equivalence which may be regarded as the consequence of polyandry. Polyandry signifies the suppression of individualism in favour of com-

---

[6]*Mahabharata*, 1,196-10.
[7]*Ibid.*, 1,104.9.

munal or fraternal tendencies. The brothers have equal opportunities and wives. In the trans-Giri the principle of equality
of brothers does not seem to have led to polyandry but was
simply a means of sustaining it. Polyandry was restricted only
to the sharing of wives, for in matters of inheritance the principles of seniority and juniority, namely jathong and kanchong,
were both applied. In the cis-Giri though the husband allowed
his brothers to have access to his wife they had no rights over
her and the husband could always check their advances or stop
their relations. Though the fraternal idea had a strong hold
and matters were decided according to the wishes of the society,
the idea of the equality of brothers was not carried very far and
jealousy was allowed to have a free scope.

It may not be out of place to mention here that the existence
of polyandry in a society which consists practically purely of
Hindus, and in a country considered sacred by the Hindus, has
created a great resentment among them and serious efforts have
been made for the eradication of this custom from the Himalayas. The movement for its eradication was started as early
as 1911 and has since been carried on. The Himalaya Vidya
Prabandhani Sabha, Simla, was the first and foremost social
organization to take the matter in hand and carry on a great
propaganda against its continuance. In 1925 Thakur Surat
Singh, General Secretary of the Sabha and a great social re-
former of the hills, devoted his energy to the eradication of
Reet and polyandry from the Himalayas and issued a pamphlet
called *Himalayan Tragedy of Marriage*. A great awakening took
place and even those affected directly by the custom could not
keep aloof. The speeches from the platform and articles in the
papers reached them directly or indirectly. As a result, the
whole social outlook has been changed and people who practise
polyandry feel ashamed of it and want to raise their status by
giving it up. Their contact with other people has convinced
them of their own degraded condition. Gradually and impercep-
tibly the practice is losing its hold on the people. Many
families which practised polyandry have given it up. The
people of trans-Giri villages near the Giri used to practise it but
due to their contact with the people of cis-Giri and other places

they have slowly given it up. In the interior of the Himalayas, such as Upper Kangra in Sirmur, Jubbal, Kumarsain, Koonawar, etc., it is still practised, not because the social outlook remains unchanged but because of the scarcity of women and the scarcity of land. It is because land in the interior cannot afford any great increase of population nor any sub-division that polyandry has continued unchecked. [Economic forces have counter-balanced all propaganda and even religious and social considerations. If it were merely a social evil, not having anything to do with economic forces, its eradication would not have been so difficult. But the social factors are so intertwined with economic considerations that in spite of a changed social outlook the practice continues. Unless the whole economic and social organization is completely overhauled the practice and habits of the people cannot be expected to undergo any great change.

To sum up, the causes of polyandry, at least as far as the Punjab Himalayas are concerned, can be divided under three separate heads: psychological, biological, and economic. Under the first head would come the traditions which have developed the mental outlook of the people. For centuries it has been dinned into their ears that the Pandavas, who were the mythical heroes of this region that still bears in its bosom memories of their exploits, had a common spouse who should be regarded as an emblem of chastity and goodness. They looked upon this institution not with shame or abhorrence but with esteem and respect. But biological and economic factors have been more powerful causes of the introduction of this practice. The scarcity of women and the birth of a greater number of male issues are significant biological factors underlying the institution of polyandry. The great difference in the number of males and females gave an undue importance and value to females which resulted not only in the introduction of polyandry but also Reet whereby women could get release from their husbands and marry others. By this custom it was also to some extent ensured that each family of brothers would, sometime or other, possess a common wife though she might not stay permanently with it. In this way the scarcity of women was made up for by the transference of females from one family to another. Reet and polyandry thus support each other. A polyandrous relation sometimes is too galling for the woman who acquires by social usage greater sexual freedom as the practice of divorce on flimsy pretexts amply shows. Nor does the biological factor of the paucity of females operate singly. It co-exists with the insuperable difficulties of framing and terracing in rocky slopes and valleys in the mist of hills. Land here is so scarce and cultivation so difficult that a holding cannot be managed successfully by an individual. The desire to leave undivided an estate on which several brothers have worked and invested their capital becomes paramount. This could only be insured through polyandry which encourages the small family habit.

Thus the interaction of biological, economic, and psychological factors has helped to keep this practice alive and, without the change in economic life and social outlook, it is not easy to forecast whether it will lose its hold on the people.

CHAPTER SEVEN

KINSHIP AND SOCIAL ORGANIZATION

Whether the family concept appears among these people as we understand it and, if so, whether they recognize the bilateral principle in their conception of family life can be deduced only from a scrutiny of their kinship and social relations and of their nomenclature. The family as a social unit includes both parents and in a secondary sense the kindred on both sides. This appears in the duties of parents to their children and also in the laws of inheritance which recognize the bond with both maternal and paternal relations.

There is no difficulty in finding the universality of the family unit in the Himalayas. Every community has terms of relationship for both the paternal and maternal lines and in so far acknowledges bilateral kinship. The two sides of the family are reckoned with not only in vocabulary but in customary law, definite functions being associated with definite types of relationship. The family takes the name of the father, *baba, bapu,* or *bao* as he is called in these communities, and not of the mother called *maan, amman,* or *ijja*. The sons of a Chauhan father and Tomar mother get the father's clan and are Chauhans and not Tomars. The family is patronymic; the wife and the children belong to the father's clan. The importance of paternal kindred is well established in society here. The movable and immovable properties descend from father to son, the father's relatives are entitled to gifts on all occasions and it is the father's kin that perform the funeral rites. But the maternal uncle has a remarkable position in the society. He plays an important part in his nephew's life. He has a voice in finding a mate for him and in the management of his marriage and receives presents by virtue of his relationship. The paternal uncle is called *kaka* while the mother's brother is called *mama*. The paternal uncle's wife is called *kakee* and the maternal uncle's wife is *mami*. The father's sister is called *booa* or *phoophee* and her husband *phoopha*, while the mother's sister is called *masi* or *mausi* and her husband *mausa*. Both paternal and maternal kindred are recognized and taking the family name of one parent does not in any way preclude important social relations with the kindred of the other.

Both parents are of course recognized; first by virtue of the sentimental bond connecting them with their children and second because the husband and wife, together with their children, form an economic and productive unit. Marriage, as we have already seen, is only to a limited extent based on sexual considerations. The primary motive is the founding of a self-sufficient economic aggregate. A man in these communities marries mainly because he needs a woman to manage his house, to look after the cattle and fodder, to bring grass and firewood, and to help him on the field while he himself attends to ploughing, harvesting, and supplying food. In this region, due to economic and sociological reasons, a man cannot always afford to maintain a separate wife for himself and so two or more husbands keep a joint wife and the children born of such a union are the property of all the husbands and they all call them fathers. The children live with them and rarely separate even when grown up. Thus the husband or husbands, wife or wives, and the children constitute a unit of the community. If a family consisting of four husbands, a wife, and two children feels at any time the necessity of another helping hand, the husbands may marry another woman and the additional wife would be submerged in the family and become a part of it without in any way disturbing its solidarity. The idea of the kin is quite strong here and a father's cousin is addressed as father though he may be quite distant in point of proximity. From him the child expects a certain mode of treatment. But the intensity of the obligation varies with the proximity of kinship. Though a number of paternal uncles and father's cousins may be addressed by the same kin term as the father, it is the father that supplies his wife and children with such necessaries as ought to be furnished by him in accordance with custom. Though a man's cousin is called brother, it is his own brother that inherits the widow through the levirate, and only in the absence of brothers does a more remote kinsman function as a substitute.

We have in the foregoing pages pointed out that the family is an unstable unit in these hills due to the peculiar conditions of the area and the scarcity of women. Both husband and wife are free to separate and divorce is very common. The presence of children does at times exert an influence on the equilibrium of marriage. After children are born the conjugal relationship becomes more stable and in long-continued unions there is loyal attachment and even deep affection. The disparity in the proportion of the sexes, the demand for woman due to her economic utility, the evils of Reet, and the uninhibited life of these hills make the family a loose unit though the changes in public opinion and social outlook of the people are slowly contributing towards stability and solidarity.

Rules of residence also exert an incalculable influence on the life of the family for physical propinquity affects not merely sexual love but all human sentiments. In this area a man looks for a mate in some village other than his own and as a rule takes his wife to his own village. He cannot generally marry in his own village because there would be his own kin in it and he cannot marry in another village and bring the wife home. His sons and unmarried daughters also live with him. A man, his brothers, and his sons with his and their wives as well as the unmarried daughters are united in one locality while the daughters who cannot marry the kinsmen of their father, on marriage follow their husbands to other villages. A man thus lives and dies in the same place while a woman spends the greater part of the life away from her natal village. This patrilocal-virilocal rule of residence establishes a male agnatic grouping of kin. There is a local segregation of individuals related through their fathers. The father has a complete voice in the management and control of the household and the mother has to carry out his wishes. When a man is not in a position to pay for his wife and serves in his prospective father-in-law's family in order to gain his daughter in marriage, he may even have to live permanently with his father-in-law and then the whole control and management of the new family unit may be different. This means that he cannot be the master of his wife's person in an absolute sense because in any dispute he has to reckon with her kin and is liable to be expelled. But such incidents are rarely met within the region for, even when the husband works as a servant of the father-in-law in order to pay for his wife, he does not stay with him after marriage but brings the wife to his own home and forms his own family there. The wife certainly has the opportunity of getting back to her parents and, if she did not want to live with her husband, would ask them to arrange for her divorce and herself choose her new mate. She cannot, however, get a release as long as she does not recompense her husband by paying the reet money and the moment she has done it she can remarry anyone of her community who is after her heart. The rule of residence is fundamentally virilocal in these hills and fathers have full control of the household and the mother and the maternal relations have very little right of interference. The unmarried boys and girls live with their parents in the same house till they are married. They are neither lodged in separate club houses or dormitories nor are they in any other respect considered as separate units of the community. We generally find a man with his brothers, his wife, and his un-married sons and daughters living under the same roof. The daughters leave the family house only when they are married, though even after marriage they visit their parents on festive occasions and bring their husbands with them. If for some reason a daughter cannot pull on with her husband she would come and stay with her parents till she has settled her quarrel with her husband or obtained divorce from him. The parents exercise very little control over her activities and she has complete liberty irrespective of the fact whether she is married or not although she has to observe discretion in her husband's house.

The husband and wife live jointly in the family house, if they have one, or in a house made by themselves. No conditions regarding segregation apply to them. They can move about freely and the husband goes very often to the fairs and other public places accompanied by his wife. The hill women are very fond of fairs and invariably accompany their husbands there in their best dress and adorned with all the ornaments they possess. With an umbrella in one hand and a cigarette in the other, she is seen following her husband in all public fairs and festivals where she can afford to go with him.

We have just considered the social relations that exist between an individual and his relatives on both his mother's and father's side. As a matter of fact, definite functions are, at times, allotted for every relationship not only of blood but of marriage as well. By legal fiction or at times by marriage even a stranger gets a definite status in a family. The system of dharam bhai is in vogue in the hills. An individual may become the dharam bhai of a boy or a girl. He would then be addressed and treated as a brother not only by the particular boy or girl who formed the relationship but his or her sisters and brothers would all address him as brother. The other relations would stand to him in the same relation as with the boy or girl who adopted him.

Certain peculiar relations with the maternal and paternal kin profoundly affect social intercourse. In a family where the mother's younger sister is likely to become the father's second wife through the sororate, the initial attitude of the children towards her is bound to be influenced by the circumstances. Similarly, the levirate creates a bond between the father's brother and his brother's son which would be absent in a different society. There are functions connected with other maternal and paternal relatives equally far-reaching in their effects.

There are usages definitely connected with the maternal and the paternal kin. In the hills the mother's brother as also the father's sister have a definite status in society. A man treats not only his mother's brother and his wife with respect but also his father's sister. Her brother and his wife would rarely perform any of the ceremonies connected with marriage without consulting her. The mother's younger sister, since she can become the second wife of the father, is held in great esteem and is treated as a mother. She is at times addressed as *choti amman* (younger mother). The mother's brother has a hand in the choice of a mate for the son and daughter. He has also to give a feast at the time of the marriage of his nephew or niece. In a Phera marriage he carries the bride to the palki or doli. He also receives presents from the bride's parents.

In the case of dissolution of marriage the girl's father and her mother's brother settle the matter for her though the boy may be represented only by his father or some other paternal kinsman. The mother's brother thus plays an important part especially as far as his niece is concerned. The nephew and the niece are in turn attached to their maternal uncle. They enjoy his hospitality whenever they want and have great liberty at his house.

There are different terms for maternal and paternal kin and each relationship carries a definite status with it. We shall briefly deal with some of the kinship terms and show how they influence social functions in Sirmur. It will be noticed that there is little difference between the kinship terms of these polyandrous people and those of a monogamous family in the plains. These terms are used practically in the whole of the region where the Baghati dialect is chiefly in vogue. There is a great similarity between the Baghati and Sirmuri dialects.

Father is addressed as Baba, Bapu, or Bao and mother as Amman, Maan or Ijja. The elder brother is called *dada* while the younger brother is called by his name. It will be found that no person who enjoys a higher status than the speaker is addressed by name. Those standing lower than him in status are called by name and that is probably why there is no special term for a younger brother. A father may call his son by name or as *beta* (son). The father's sister is called phoophee and her husband phoopha. The father's younger brother is called *kaka* and the father's younger brother's wife is called *kakee*. The father's father is called *nana* and the father's mother *nanee*. Similarly, the mother's father is called nana and the mother's mother nanee. In many communities, in the cis-Giri and in the plains, the father's father is called *dada* and the father's mother *dadee*. It is only the mother's father and the mother's mother who are called nana and nanee respectively. It is only in the interior trans-Giri tract of Sirmur that we find the same kinship terms for the father's father and the mother's father. While a person succeeds to his father's father's property immediately on his death if his own father be not alive and has a right in his paternal grandfather's property as soon as he is born, he does not have the same rights in his mother's father's property. A sister is called *bobo* or *jijjee*. The rule of incest is very strictly followed in the case of brother and sister, mother and son, father and daughter. The sister's husband is called *jija*. He stands in an absolutely different status. He can have liberties with his *sali* or *salis*, his wife's sisters, as the younger sali can be wedded to him according to sororate. In families where polyandry is not practised, the brother's wife enjoys a peculiar status. She is inherited on her husband's death by her husband's brother. She is, therefore, his potential mate. Her husband's brother has practically the same rights over her as a *jija* over his sali. He freely meets her and his taking liberties with her is not resented. Even a younger brother's widow can be married which shows that senior levirate is practised here. Thus licensed familiarity generally prevails between potential mates. A brother-in-law's wife is addressed as a sister and treated as such in these parts. They respect each other and do not take any liberties. Quite different relations, however, exist between a man's sister's husband's sister and himself. He can cut jokes with her and no taboos apply to them. The mother's sister is called mausi and her husband mausa. She is greatly respected by her nephews and nieces and is the potential mate of their father, if she is their mother's younger sister.

The mother's brother is called mama and his wife mamee. The husband's father is called *shohra* (in Kangra; in Sirmur he is also called mama) while the husband's mother is called *sasu*. A Sirmur bride thus calls her husband's father and her mother's brother by the same term mama. Mama in the ordinary sense signifies the mother's brother. We have in this case one term for two different relationships. This suggests that the bride's mother and her husband's father might be sister and brother. In other words, the bride might be her husband's father's sister's daughter, i.e. a cross-cousin marriage might be expected here and on investigation it was found to be true. The wife's mother, like the husband's mother, is called sasu and the wife's father shohra. The wife's mother and the husband's mother are held in great respect and no liberties are taken with them. A son is called beta and a daughter *betee.* A daughter's husband is called *jawaeen,* a daughter's son *dohta,* and her daughter *dohtee.* A son's wife is called *bahu,* a son's son *pota,* and a son's daughter *potee.* A brother's son is called *bhaicha* and sister's son *bhanja.* A brother's daughter is called *bhaichi* (from *bhaiya* or brother) and a sister's daughter *bhanji.*

There are the various kinship terms used in the hills. These apply not only to the near but also to the distant kin and at times are bewildering to a stranger. An illustration may make the point clear. A person would apply the term kaka not only to his father's brother but even to the latter's most distant cousins on the paternal side. Thus a person will have a number of kakas who have in fact very little to do with the family. Similarly, the mother's brother would be called mama and all the cousins of the latter on the paternal side would also be addressed as mama. But the social obligations of the near kin are different from those of the distant kin and though one owes the same type of conduct to a more remote as to a closer kinsman and though both are addressed by the same relationship term, the intensity of obligation is greater for the nearer relationship. Thus while father's every cousin would be a kaka it is only one's father's brother who has to take up the management of the household and give protection to one's mother on one's father's death. The distant kinsmen have no such obligations and they have any only when nearer kinsmen do not exist.

A study of kinship terms and usages may also be of help to us in considering the matter of inheritance and succession. We have seen that polygyny and polyandry are both practised side by side in these hills. The existence of these practices at the same time moulds the laws of inheritance in a peculiar but interesting manner. Ordinarily the courts of law follow the Benares School of Mitakshara law as far as inheritance and succession are concerned but the local customs hold their own and in case of any difference the local custom is a decisive factor. Succession does not, as it does in other parts of India, offer any great intricacies here. The simple life of the inhabitants has developed a system of succession suitable to their local needs. None of the complexities and subtleties of the Hindu succession are present and few persons have to approach the courts in this connection. The problems of partition and inheritance of the joint family property are scarcely present. The reason for their absence is the simple fact that the family is for all practical purposes one solid unit and is hardly ever divisible especially as far as a polyandrous family is concerned. A number of brothers marry one joint wife. The offsprings by the common wife are the sons or daughters of the family. In a polyandrous family, on the death of a brother his sons do not inherit his property if his other brothers are living. A brother succeeds a brother and only when all the brothers are dead do their children inherit the property. Since the sons in a polyandrous family are considered to be the offspring of all the fathers they cannot become fatherless till all the brothers are dead. The sons have in turn to remain joint and to get a joint wife not only for social reasons but also for economic necessity. These factors do not afford the members of the family any opportunity or inducement for a division of the property or for separation. Even in families which practise polygyny succession does not produce any complications. All the male issues of the wives are heirs to their father's property. The property on the death of the father at once passes on to the male issues. It is divided equally among them. The sons of any particular wife do not get any extra share. If, however, a man dies without any male issue, property is equally divided amongst his wives who have only a life-interest in the property. The widows do not have the authority to dispose of the immovable property by will, gift or sale. On their death it will pass on to the nearest collaterals. We shall now deal briefly with inheritance as it is practised in the different localities in the Himalayas, especially those where polyandry is prevalent.

In Bashahr, as in most of the adjoining region, inheritance goes per stirpes and not per capita. The right of the children born from a regular *biah*, i.e. a formal marriage, is considered superior to that of all others. A well-to-do man may have four kinds of children: (*i*) by a formally married wife; (*ii*) by a Jhajra or Gadar wife; (*iii*) by Serteras, i.e. an irregular marriage with a woman of lower caste than his own; and (*iv*) *Jhatas*, i.e. children by a purely adulterous connection. On his death the children by the wife married according to the formal ceremony of marriage get one half and in some places two-thirds of his property. The remainder is divided amongst the other children in shares fixed by the members of the father's brotherhood. Inheritance in Sirmur, as we shall see later, goes per capita and not per stirpes. The jhatas as a rule become servants to the rest of the family and are supported by them; or else are given a field or two and a small sum of money. If partition has to be carried out by any group of children it is done according to the rule of jathong and kanchong. In the case of a polyandrous family all the sons succeed the father but remain joint. If one of the brothers dies his sons and widow do not succeed him but he is succeeded by his younger brother or brothers. Only when all the brothers are dead their sons inherit the property. All the sons now have a joint interest and ownership and, if they want to separate, the eldest and youngest brothers have to be given separate extra shares in accordance with the rule of jathong and kanchong.

If a widow remarries, in or outside the husband's family, she is not entitled to his property. In the case of a polyandrous family the question of widowhood or remarriage would not arise so long as one of the husbands is living. It is only when all the joint husbands are dead that a wife becomes a widow in a polyandrous family. If she remarries she loses her right in that family and is not entitled to its property.

The rules of inheritance in respect of polyandrous families in the Simla district are the same as in Bashahr.

Inheritance in the Kangra district does not show any great difference though slight variations may be noticed. In Kangra,

as in Bashahr and Sirmur, the *jetha beta* (eldest son) gets something as jethanda in addition to the share which he inherits
equally with other sons. This jethanda is the same as the jathong
which we find in Bashahr state and Sirmur state. This extra
share may consist of a field, a cow or an ox or any other
movable but valuable commodity. In the case of inheritance of
sons by more than one wife the Chundavand and not the
Pagvand rule is followed. In the Chundavand rule the inheritance is based on the number of mothers and not on the
number of sons.

Legitimacy is a condition of inheritance and if a son be not
considered legitimate he is debarred from inheritance. The
landholders may be put into two classes in this district. First,
those whose women observe seclusion and do not work in the
fields and who do not practise jhanjrara or widow marriage and
secondly, those who marry widows and allow their women to
work in the fields.

In the case of the former the son of a Rakhorar wife would
be a *sirtora* (illegimate). A son by a *Rakhorar* ("kept" woman)
is not considered legitimate and inherits no share. Among the
latter class the son of a kept woman, provided she is not of im-
pure caste and connection with her does not involve loss of caste,
would inherit equally with the sons by a wife married formally
because in such a case a Jhanjrara marriage would be presumed.

Sons begotten by a first husband, called *Pichlags*, who accompany their mother to her second husband's house are not
entitled to any share in the latter's property though he may
treat them as his own. But the Gaddis and lower castes appear
to hold the view that if a man takes as wife a widow who is at
the time in the family way, the child born should be reckoned
his child and not a Pichlag. Due to the scarcity of children even
a Kanet may at times do so but it is looked upon with disfavour and may even cause quarrel and litigation.

A widow has a right to inherit her husband's property on
his death. She holds the property only for life and on her death
it reverts to the nearest collateral of her husband. She holds
the property for life on the condition of chastity. If she loses
her chastity she loses her right of inheritance. But the Kanet's

Giraths, and other lower castes do not take this view. They hold that as long as a widow continues to live at her husband's house she is entitled to his property. She may be openly carrying on with a man but as long as she is in her husband's house she does not lose her right. The moment she gives up her house to live with someone else she is deprived of her right of inheritance.

In Kullu, Saraj, Lahaul and Spiti, however, the rules of inheritance vary a little from those of Kangra district proper. The children of a Brahman or Rajput by a Kanet wife are called Brahmans or Rajputs. In the absence of other children they are their father's full-heirs. In the presence of other children by a *lari* (formally wedded wife) they would only get a share by way of maintenance put by some at one-fifth. In Kullu the rule of inheritance is Pagavand or, as it is called in Kullu, Mundevand. All the legitimate sons of a father get equal shares whatever be the number of sons born of each wife, as in Kangra. The Kanets and lower castes are not very strict about the matter of legitimacy as affecting inheritance. Even a son by a kept woman would be considered legitimate and would inherit the property of his father. It is not necessary that his father should have performed any formal ceremony of marriage with his mother but if his mother has been living as a wife with his father, that would be considered enough to bestow legitimacy on him. In the same way a Pichlag or a posthumous son, called *Ronda* in Kullu, born to a widow in the house of her second husband is considered the son of the second husband. A widow would not be deprived of her life-interest in her husband's estate for want of chastity, among these communities in Kullu, as long as she does not go away to live in another man's house. In Kullu a father may give away his property to his daughter by way of gift if he had no son. He must, however, execute a deed of gift for the purpose though the consent of the collaterals is not required. It is only the nearest of kin who have the right to question an alienation by a father in favour of his daughter by way of gift and it is doubtful if distant kinsmen can put forward claims against such a daughter without a properly executed gift. A *ghar-jawaee* (a son-in-law who lives with his in-laws) often becomes entitled to succeed as a kind of adopted son without proof of gift or formal ceremony. In the case of subordinate land-holders, all sons are entitled to equal shares in the father's property. In practice, they seldom divide but live on with wife, land house, and chattel in common. In Pattan, the Hindu element predominates and holdings too are larger and more productive. Some brothers have married there separately and have divided house and land. On the whole, however, separations and partitions are not common.

If a brother dies without issue no difficulty arises as to the inheritance of his property. His share would pass to the brothers with whom he lived jointly, to the exclusion of all claims on the part of the separated branch of the family. An exceptional point in the custom of inheritance prevailing in Lahaul is the fact that in the absence of sons a daughter succeeds to her father's whole estate in preference to nephews or other male kinsmen provided that she has not married and settled down to live on her husband's holdings away from her home before her father's death. If she is married and is living with her husband in her father's house she succeeds, and if she is unmarried, she can hold the property for life as a maid or can at any time marry and make her husband live with her. But if she does not live there she has to forego her right in the father's property. If such a husband and wife die without issue while living on the property of the wife's father it is not clear who would have the best claim to succeed them, whether the next of kin to the wife or to the husband. But this much is clear that any of the survivors may lawfully give the property to any member of the two families.

We shall now take up the working of the rules of inheritance in Sirmur area. In families where polygyny is practised succession does not present any complications. All the male issues are heirs to their father's property. The property on the death of the father at once passes on to them. It is divided equally among them. The sons of any particular wife do not get any preference. The property is divided per capita and not per stirpes. If a man dies without any male issue, the property would be equally divided amongst his wives who have only a life interest in it. The widows have not the authority to dispose of the immovable property. On their death it will pass on to the nearest collaterals.

In a family which practises polyandry, a brother, as already stated, inherits from a brother as long as partition is not made. Among the brothers the wives cannot often be equally divided. If, for instance, there are four brothers and they have only two wives the division becomes rather difficult. In such a case the two eldest or any other two brothers in whose name the two wives were brought keep them while the other two who do not get wives are compensated in cash. They are thus all given equal opportunities. Immovable property is divided according to each brother's share.

Families which are monogamous differ a little in matters of succession. Where each brother possesses a wife and the brothers separate, the method of division and succession is a little different. On the death of a person, his brothers do not inherit the immovable property so long as his widow is living. The widow gets a life-interest in the property. As long as she lives in his house she is the owner of the property of her dead husband. In case she remarries she loses her interest in it. If she forms an illicit connection with someone while under the roof of her husband and an illegitimate child is born, the child, if it is a male one, is considered to be her husband's son though born years after his death and shall inherit her husband's property. But such cases are rare. As far as movable property is concerned, she is the absolute owner and may dispense with it as she likes. Sons by a woman who is kept as a wife, but for whom no Reet money has been paid or with whom the formal ceremony of marriage has not been gone through, generally inherit their father's property. This custom has been contested but is generally accepted.

We find some difference between the rules of inheritance in Kangra, Simla hills, and Sirmur. In Sirmur a woman of a lower caste, who is kept as a concubine, is not a lawful wife and her sons do not inherit while such sons get at least a maintenance in Kangra and the Simla hill states.

A man by marrying a woman of a lower caste sinks to that

caste. As we have already seen, the only exception to the rule is the intermarriage of Bhats and Kanets. But a Bhat or Kanet marrying a Kolan becomes a Koli. If a Koli marries a Kanetni he will not be an outcast but the Kanetni will become a Kolan and out-casted by the Kanets. This does not affect succession in any way because marriage with a woman of a higher caste is allowed by society. Both in trans-Giri and cis-Giri, a man who marries a woman of a lower caste as well as his descendants cannot inherit from his collaterals if the latter die without heirs. Such a man is generally excommunicated. There is some difference of opinion as to whether he can hold the ancestral property or not. If the ancestral property is undivided at the time of his marriage with a woman of a lower caste, he cannot inherit any immovable property. If, however, partition has taken place and he has got possession of his share, he is allowed to keep it till his death. On his death his sons do not inherit it and it reverts to his collaterals.

In the lower classes only in Sirmur a Pichlag or a posthumous child born in the house of a woman's second husband is entitled to succeed to his mother's second husband. The bulk of the population does not recognize the class of Sarteras, as people do in Kangra, for a son by any form of marriage is considered legitimate. It is only in the ruling family that this class is to be had in Sirmur. The members of the ruling family who are Rajputs take Kanet or Bhat girls as servants. While they are denied the status of wives, they are subject to sexual connection with their masters and are called khwases. Nor formal marriage ceremony is performed with them though Reet money is often paid for them. Male issues by such women are called Sarteras. But while children by such connections would be considered legitimate by the people and would inherit the property of their father, it is strange that the Sarteras are not considered legitimate and have no right in their father's property but merely get maintenance from their father or his successor. It is the only class of offspring in Sirmur and the Simla hill states which cannot by birth acquire any right in the property of the father and has to depend for its livelihood on the mercy of the progenitors. Sarteras are in the same condition throughout the Simla hill states and Tehri state. While because of their connections with the ruling family they consider themselves of a superior rank their position is not happy in society.

Daughters do not inherit their father's immovable property in the trans-Giri tract. If there are no collaterals up to the seventh degree, a daughter's son or in his absence a sister's son inherits the property. But both in trans-Giri and cis-Giri, the father or brother of a girl can give a part of the landed property to her in charity. In this case there should be a written deed of gift which should have the consent of the collaterals. But the father or brother can give the girl a part of the landed property with a life-interest only without any written document. The nearest collaterals, i.e. the father or brother, can also give a moiety of the landed property to the daughter or sister as dowry at the time of her marriage.

A man cannot adopt a child except from his own caste. It is not quite certain whom one can adopt. The *Sirmur Gazetteer* states that a man must prefer one from his family or among his collaterals to any other member of the same caste. But on investigation in the trans-Giri tract it was found that he is not bound to prefer his collaterals. A widow cannot generally adopt but she can do it with the consent of the collaterals of her husband.

The *Sufa* (the right of pre-emption) is also found among these people. Sufa is the right possessed by the owner of certain immovable property to acquire by purchase certain other immovable property in preference to others. The person entitled to this right is called a *shuftee* (pre-emptor). The right of pre-emption in village communities in India had its origin in the Mohammadan law, and was apparently unknown in India before the time of the Moghul rulers. Pre-emption can take place only in case of sale and not mortgage.

The making of a will when a man or a woman possesses issues is unknown. Even if a father is not on good terms with his sons he will not ordinarily make a will in regard to his personal property to deprive his son of it. It is only when there is no male issue that one resorts to a will. A man as well as a widow can make a will after taking the consent of the collaterals.

The institution of charity and gift finds a place in the civil code of these people. One may give away a part of his immovable property by way of charity. This shall have to be entered in the patwari or village accountant's register. A widow who has inherited property from her husband may make a gift of a small portion of the immovable property which she has received from her husband.

CHAPTER EIGHT

CHANGES IN MARRIAGE LAW
AND CUSTOM

In this chapter I have described the changes in marriage law and custom which took place during the days of the feudal rulers in the region. These changes were initiated by a process of acculturation which was rather slow in the hills due to their isolated situation and by the legislative measures taken by the erstwhile princely states in their kingdoms. It was therefore not surprising that few changes in the social sphere were discernible. Nevertheless, western influence was colouring public opinion and changing the social outlook so that readjustments took place in the life of the people and in their marriage laws and customs.

The people of the region did realize their backwardness and and also that their customs were not in strict conformity with the orthodox Hindu code. The people, due to scarcity of land and meagreness of livelihood, could no longer afford to stick to their homes. Those of them who had a touch of the spirit of adventure went out to earn their living in Simla and other towns. A number of porters in Simla were residents of the neighbouring Simla hill states and Sirmur. The Rickshaw coolies in Simla were mostly residents of Kangra, many of them being Rajputs. Their contact with districts where the social and economic life of the people is very different was bound to affect their angle of vision and outlook on life. They realized that they must adopt new customs and practices and give up some of the old ones in order to come in line with more advanced groups.

The Jhajra or Jhanjtara form of marriage is still very common in the region. As already noted, Jhajra as they have it in Sirmur and the Jhanjara of Kangra are in some respects different from each other. No formal ceremonies were originally necessary in the case of a Jhajra form of marriage. Bedi and Shant ceremonies are not known to have been performed in Jhajra nor did people understand what they mean. But Bedi and Shant were introduced during these years and were generally adopted. The phera ceremony was not known in the trans-Giri tract of Sirmur and in the Simla hills, particularly in the interior. Only in places which were near the headquarters of a state or some district, marriages took place according to the phera. But in the trans-Giri tract and in other parts of the Simla hills phera became popular. The well-to-do families married according to the phera and other people too, in many cases, adjusted it to a Jhajra marriage. There was a tendency to give a more orthodox shape to marriage and minor changes were brought about by the introduction of the phera. The dress also underwent a transformation. The ordinary wedding dress for a bride used to consist of an *angulta* (like a blouse) and *ghaghtu* (a skirt up to the knees only) and a *dhartu* (a large handkerchief tied round the head to serve as a head dress). In Sirmur, the dhartu used to be generally white in colour but in Jubbal state and Mandi state the black colour was more in fashion. The black colour was adopted in Sirmur too for it seems to suit the fair hill women more than the white. The angulta was now practically superseded (except in the case of old women who still put it on) by kurta or shirt, the ghagtu by pyjamas, and the dhartu by a chaddar or head cover. In the trans-Giri tract of Sirmur, the bride did not don any coloured clothes in the past but she used to put on white clothes only. She now puts on coloured clothes.

Some of the expensive customs were also modified and the people ceased to be such spendthrifts as they used to be in the past. One can very well realize the extent of their extravagance when one finds that in the past a decent wedding party used to consist of 500 to 1,000 persons. It is not an easy matter to entertain such a huge party even in the simplest manner. But they were to be served with meat and rice, or rice, sugar and ghee. The result was that the people had to borrow money.

While the resources of the people were attenuated, they learnt from contact with the outside world that this expenditure was a waste. They came to realize its absurdity and a much smaller number of men, rarely 300 persons in all, were taken in a wedding party. Thus the expenditure on marriage and on other ceremonial occasions was reduced though one cause of poverty, the Reet or bride price, had not yet been removed.

The attitude to polyandry also underwent a change and it was no longer held in that esteem which it enjoyed two decades back. The efforts of the social reformers and the pressure of public opinion forged a new angle of vision for the people. Their contact with orthodox society and the treatment which was meted out to them because of this objectionable practice had their effects on their mind. They now realized that they should discard it. Some of them, who could afford it, gave it up. In the outlying parts people did not practise it and those who did were reluctant to acknowledge it. But their economic and social conditions were such that they could not afford to give it up completely and at once. But where circumstances permitted the custom was given up and its place was gradually taken up by monandry. When possible, brothers separated and, if they could afford it, had separate wives who were exclusively the wives of their husbands. Even where polyandry and polygyny were practised side by side, the tendency was to have a wife exclusively for oneself. The desire for a change was evident and whenever possible polyandry was discarded.

The working of Reet in the region had also undergone some modification. It affected the life of the people and resulted in their indebtedness. On the whole the marriage tie in the hills was very loose. Where polyandry was not practised it was common for a wife to cohabit freely with her husband's brothers. Marriage had no stability and a woman could leave her husband and find out another mate any time and as often as she pleased. Family solidarity was completely shaken and a serious problem faced the hillman. The custom of Reet provided the women with a handy and effective weapon and they used their position to their heart's content. Attempts were made by some of the Simla hill states to stop this custom by legislation. The social reformers and some public organizations did all they could to carry on an intensive propaganda against this custom. The Rajput Sthania Sabha, the Vidya Prabandhini Sabha, and the Hindu Conference, Simla, brought this subject to the forefront of public attention and approached the highest authorities for its suppression. Some states did take active steps to make marriage a more stable institution and give it a sanctity which it lacked at the time.

The first state to legislate on Reet was the Patiala Darbar in whose territories in the hills this custom was rampant. A circular (No. 12, 23 November 1912) was issued by the Judicial Department, Patiala State, as follows:

It is hereby ordered in compliance with the orders of His Highness the Maharaja Saheb Bahadur G.C.I.E., that the vicious custom of Rit, prevalent in the hill tracts of Patiala State, should be discontinued. The local officers in the hill territories are therefore directed to exert their influence in the suppression of Rit and not to recognise the same officially.

They are further directed to supply six-monthly figures, as far as possible, to show what progress has been made in the suppression of this custom.

This legislation, however, remained a dead letter and very little was done to give effect to it. One of the prominent Delhi nationalist papers commenting on this legislation said: "Some 13 years ago, the Maharaja of Patiala issued an order prohibiting marriages by Reet within the tract of his own State and refused it judicial recognition. Six-monthly reports of the progress which might be made were also ordered to be sent up to him. We would like to know how far this prohibitory order has really remained a dead letter."[1]

The Patiala State, however, refused to give official recognition to the custom. Reet marriage could no longer be considered a valid marriage. The state, however, helped the public by registering marriages and charging a nominal registration fee. If any-

[1] *The Hindustan Times*, 28 May 1925.

one married according to Reet he would get a bond from his wife and have it registered. The contract would bind the parties and unless the husband released the woman after taking proper compensation as Reet she would remain his wife and the deed would establish his claim. The custom was thus in practice in a modified form in Patiala but its working was not materially affected.

The second to legislate in this matter was a Highland Chief of Bhagat state, the late Sir Rana Dalip Singh Bahadur, C.I.E. He framed a certain legislation, published it in a treatise, and enforced it in his state. The first three sections run as follows:

(*i*) This Act shall be called the "Abolition of Rit Custom" and shall come into force in the State with effect from the 23rd July, 1917.

(*ii*) Anyone who shall infringe this law, on or after the 23rd July, 1917, shall be punished within the provision of this Act.

(*iii*) To marry a woman by Rit is forbidden. Neither man nor woman whose husband is alive shall become another man's wife by Rit. No man shall keep as wife any woman whose husband is alive. Whoever will commit breach of these provisions shall be punished under Sections 497, 498, 363, 366, 496, 494 of the Indian Penal Code and any one proved to be an accomplice in a Rit affair shall be liable to be prosecuted under Act XV of 1856.

But the result was far from satisfactory. *The Hindustan Times* (28 May 1925) expressed its disapproval of the measure as adopted in practice. It said:

The Ruler of Bhagat State took a severer step and enacted a law for the abolition of the custom of Reet, making it an offence punishable under various sections of the Indian Penal Code. The Government of India also issued a prohibitory order some years ago but to no purpose. The various Governments must, we feel, come under the charge of merely tinkering with the problem. A much more vigorous and better co-ordinated campaign is urgently called for, if this ugly fossil of bygone ages is not still to disfigure Indian social life and devitalize the useful hill tribes of the Himalayas. The Indian Government, the Rulers of the Hill States and the social reformers of the tract must combine to concert and adopt measures for the abolition of the evil custom, and bring the marriage laws of these tribes in a line with the rest of the country.

The Jubbal state authorities gave the custom their own colouring and though the social evils with which it was associated were not checked the economic consequences were to a great extent controlled. No fresh Reet marriages were to take place and only those husbands who had paid Reet for wives would be entitled to receive Reet from the parents of the wife and not from the subsequent husband and only the Reet originally paid, and Rs 25 at most as compensation, could be realized. This order upset the working of Reet for a time for people had paid huge sums of money, rupees hundred or more, for a woman and paid interest thereon and, now that it was their turn to have compensation when their wives left them, they could not receive more than the principal. On the whole, however, it had a very healthy effect on the masses. The people could not in fact afford the huge sums they were required to pay and found it necessary to borrow money in order to pay Reet. Once indebted, the family would always be so and indebtedness had become perpetual in family life. Ever since Reet was checked in this manner the financial position of the people improved and one of the most important causes of indebtedness had been removed. But it was only within Jubbal that this rule applies. If a Jubbal woman was to marry someone in Sirmur or any other neighbouring state according to Reet the husband paid according to the custom of his own land. I met husbands from Sirmur and other neighbouring states who had married Jubbal women according to Reet and have had to pay a sum between Rs 100 and Rs 400 for them. On being questioned about it, the parents of the girl replied that Jubbal legislation applied to parties who belonged to Jubbal only. This legislation affected their financial condition and the stability of their marriage. The women had less inducement to make a change and the wealthy and rich who tempted them were denied the special attraction of paying huge sums of money for them. On the whole Jubbal state seemed to have taken a beneficial step regarding Reet as far as the masses of Jubbal were concerned. It discouraged the frequent change of husbands and removed a vital cause of the indebtedness of the people. It also absolved itself of the charge which was levelled at that time that the states were interested in making profit out of the wretched position of the people. The state no longer derived any income out of it and an inducement was offered to the people to discontinue the customs.

The Sirmur Darbar also paid a good deal of attention to this matter. It was probably one of the first to take action against this custom. It was as far back as 1885 A.D. that the Sirmur Darbar took active steps in checking this custom by levying a 5 per cent tax on it. The tax was increased from 5 per cent to 7 per cent in 1886, to 10 per cent in 1890, and finally in 1910 to 15 per cent. Though the Reet tax was raised from 5 to 15 per cent the custom was not checked but received an impetus from it. The very object with which the tax had been levied was frustrated. It originally applied only to those women whose husbands were alive and the hillmen. Gradually it was applied to the widows as well, who had been specially exempted from its operation and then Banias, Banjaras, etc., also came within its ambit. Every care was taken to safeguard against a breach of the rules and also to ensure realization of the tax. While the returns from the tax went on increasing every year, as the table on the facing page shows, and amounted to Rs 36,000 in 1920, the custom of Reet went on unchecked and its hold over the people was stronger than it had ever been before.

It had become patent to all that the tax had defeated its very object and instead of checking the evil had offered it an inducement. The people wanted to get out of its shackles but they could not though they brought its evil effects to the notice of the authorities.

Year (A.D.)	Rate of Reet tax	Return in rupees
1899	7 per cent	3,000
1902	10 ,, ,,	5,000
1903	10 ,, ,, (widows also taxed)	10,000
1904	10 per cent	5,000
1909	10 ,, ,,	7,000
1910	15 ,, ,,	9,000
1911	15 ,, ,,	13,000
1915	15 ,, ,,	19,000
1920	15 ,, ,,	36,000
1921	15 ,, ,,	32,000
1922	,, ,, ,,	30,911
1923	,, ,, ,,	25,576
1924	,, ,, ,,	33,800
1925	,, ,, ,,	32,230
1926	,, ,, ,,	34,263
1927	,, ,, ,,	26,948
1928	,, ,, ,,	25,574
1929	,, ,, ,,	30,605
1930	,, ,, ,,	21,499
1931	,, ,, ,,	11,443
1932	,, ,, ,,	13,539
1933	,, ,, ,,	12,551
1934	,, ,, ,,	12,485
1935	,, ,, ,,	14,872
1936	,, ,, ,,	18,681
1937	,, ,, ,,	23,607
1938	,, ,, ,,	21,832

It were not the rulers alone who had given careful consideration to this custom but individuals and associations of the hills
also did so and carried on a vigorous propaganda for its abolition. Substantial work in this connection was done by the
Himalaya Vidya Prabandhini Sabha, Simla, which volunteered
its services for the cause of the people of the hills. It convened
small gatherings, started propaganda work, issued pamphlets,
and tried its best to root out this evil. In a letter to the
Superintendent, Simla Hill States, the Secretary of the Sabha
in 1924 wrote that some of the Chiefs of the hill states seemed

to have suffered Reet to continue unchecked perhaps because of the handsome income they derive by way of the percentage they levied on the sale money of the women. This percentage was intended to serve as a deterrent to the custom by imposing additional liability on the party concerned but was now looked upon as no more than a tax, like several others, leviable by, and due to, the state. The Sabha passed a resolution stating that no woman should marry in her husband's lifetime. It appealed to the government to penalize this custom as the people were incapable of putting a stop to it themselves as in the case of Sati and infanticide.

The Sabha submitted a proposal to insert a provision in the Indian Penal Code dealing with "Barda-Faroshi" and to amend Section 361 of the Code to raise the age of marriage in the case of boys from 14 to 16. It also addressed a letter to the Deputy Commissioner, Simla, on 1 August 1924, suggesting that the proposed legislation should provide for the following:

(a) The definition of "Barda-Farosh" should be worded wide enough so as to include father, brother or husband of a girl or whoever sells her not for bonafide purposes but ostensibly for illicit intercourse and free latitude of marriage.

(b) Provision should be made for declaring liable to punishment any person who procures a married or unmarried girl either for the sake of remarrying her or of passing her on to another person for similar purpose.

(c) Purchase of a girl for employment as household servant or for purposes of giving her away in dowry as a "Khawas" or maid servant with a bride should be prohibited.

The cause taken up by the Sabha found support in the Hindu Conference, Simla district, which was held in 1924 in Simla. Among others the following resolution was passed at the Conference : "(9) That the custom of Reet which prevails in the Hills, being the root cause of the degraded condition of the people of the Hills, their poverty and misery, and of the depletion of the population and being contrary to Shastras, the Rulers and Chiefs of Hill States and the Deputy Commissioner and the Agent to the Governor-General, Punjab states, in whose jurisdiction the evil custom prevails, be requested to put it down by appropriate legislation. The Hindu community would feel grateful to them for the boon."

One more important resolution was passed by the Conference which affected this custom. It ran as follows: "That the Conference is of opinion that the decrees of the courts of Ruling Chiefs of Hill States in the matter of restitution of conjugal rights should be recognised and enforced by British Indian Courts, and that decrees of the British Indian Courts be recognised and enforced by the courts of the Ruling Chiefs of the hill States; that the non-recognition of such decrees is a source of great hardship and social mischief to the people."

CHAPTER NINE

MODERNIZATION AND SOCIAL CHANGE

This chapter discusses the great transformation that has taken place in the hill tracts which now constitute the state of Himachal Pradesh which was formed in 1948 as an administrative unit of the Indian Union. The great political, economic, and developmental activities since then have immensely transformed the whole social structure of this region and consequently the age-old customs, values, and social institutions have also undergone a tremendous change.

POLITICAL CHANGES

The social history of Himachal Pradesh, prior to its formation in 1948 as one administrative unit, is the story of numerous remotely situated hamlets, isolated and scattered over vast area and ruled by different feudal rajas (chieftains). Separated by high mountain-ranges, deep gorges, innumerable streams and rivers, and varying administrative set-ups the people here strangely enough preserved their cultural unity for centuries. The tumult of the plains below had left them untouched and they, for ages, lived a life their forefathers had lived. Their faiths were unadultrated, their customs deep-rooted, and their outlook happy. They struggled hard against vagaries of nature to eke out a living, and believed their existence to be fated that way. Their day long fatigue was drowned in the festivity of the song and dance at night. Fairs, functions, and festivals provided them an outlet for rejoicing. Having nothing much to spend, they were dazzled by the shopping available for the higher classes in the innumerable fairs where the feudal lords and big landowners participated with great pomp. Though suffering, they ungrudgingly gave everything to their god and the raja who was also called *deva* (god) in some areas. No doubt there were revolts here and there against the feudal rajas, but they had the protection of the British empire and always succeeded in quelling them.

Life apparently went on peacefully, despite the seething discontent under the surface on account of *begar* (forced labour), unequal laws between classes, and overall suppression. The awakening in the rest of India and the struggle for freedom in the country did not leave the hills absolutely untouched. Getting inspiration from the All-India States People's Conference, Praja Mandals were organized for the attainment of democratic rights for the people in most of the princely states, in some places openly and in some secretly.

Late thirties and early forties of the century were trying years for the freedom fighters who had to carry on the struggle from within and outside the princely states that now comprise Himachal Pradesh. Terror was unleashed in some states and the Praja Mandal workers were subjected to untold sufferings. Some were extradited and their properties confiscated—the author was one of them. Communications being negligible, the story of naked suppression let loose hardly reached the outside world. Even the exchange of notes by freedom fighters in different states was not easily possible as no roads or other channels of communications were available. At places the movement was a joint one, but in most states it grew in isolation. Towards the close of the Second World War, the struggle for the liberation of areas from feudal yoke gained momentum. The echo of India, being at the threshold of independence in 1946, shook many a princely citadel. New efforts were made by the rulers to bypass the upsurge that was gaining ground every day. Some reforms here or there were introduced and democratization of administration attempted, but it was more to divert public attention than to give them anything of real substance. India achieved independence on 15 August 1947, and with the transfer of power from the British Crown to India's representatives, the position of princely states vis-a-vis people completely changed.

Each princely state was in political ferment. People could no longer be kept under feudal tyranny. Groups of Praja

Mandal workers formed in different states started merging. The struggle no longer remained on individual basis; it became collective and general. The wind of freedom started blowing over the hilly areas. On 26 January 1948, a resolution moved by the author at a public meeting held in Simla (now Capital of Himachal Pradesh) urging upon national leadership to integrate the Simla hill states and form a state of hilly areas was passed unanimously. It was also on this day that the Himalayan Prant Provisional Government was formed and the struggle for the merger of princely states entered its final phase.

On 18 February 1948, about a thousand Praja Mandal satyagrahis marched into Suket (a state situated between the two states of Mandi and Bilaspur) when its ruler did not respond to the 48-hour notice given to him for merging his state with the Indian Union. As the march continued, hundreds of more people joined it. Police posts fell and the tehsil head-quarters were occupied without any resistance. People every-where gave the satyagrahis a big welcome. Within six days, three-fourths of the Suket state came under the Provisional Government.

The fall of Suket state made rulers of other princely states read the writing on the wall and one after the other they sought to sign the instrument of merger with the Indian Union. On 15 April 1948, 30 hill states of Chamba, Mandi, Suket, Bashahr, Khaneti, Delath, Keonthal, Koti, Theog, Madhan, Ghund, Ratesh, Baghal, Jubbal, Rawin, Dhadi, Baghat, Kumar-sain, Bhajji, Mehlog, Balson, Dhami, Kuthar, Kunihar, Mangal, Beja, Darkoti, Tharoch, Sangri, and Sirmur were merged to form Himachal Pradesh as a Chief Commissioner's Province with a population of 9,35,000 and an area of 10,600 sq. miles.

In 1952, Himachal Pradesh became a Part 'C' state of the Indian Union with a Lieutenant-Governor, a Legislative Assembly, and a popular ministry. Simultaneously, its first five-year plan was launched. By this time, it had completed about four years of its existence, but excepting the new awaken-ing and consciousness among the people about their rights, no substantial change was evident in its social and economic structure. It was during the period of the first popular ministry that social and economic reforms of far-reaching consequences were introduced transforming the entire life of the Pradesh. Moreover, the development works undertaken in the fields of road construction, education and health accelerated the process of change.

The year 1956 was one of great apprehension and unrest for the people of Himachal Pradesh. The States Reorganization Commission, set up by the Government of India, submitted its report early in this year. Its majority verdict recommended that Himachal should be merged with the neighbouring state of Punjab, while its Chairman, Fazal Ali, argued that "in small states the administration will be accessible to people; and there will be livelier sense of local need," and therefore, Himachal should not be merged with Punjab. The entire atmosphere was charged with uncertainty and all was at stake for the people of Himachal. They had only a few years ago got rid of the feudal rule and now they were frightened with the ugly prospect of undergoing domination from the plains of Punjab, if their Pradesh was merged with that state. In the merger, they saw a danger to their cultural and social life and a threat to their emerging economy which was sure to be yoked to the economic exigencies of the plains.

Being small in numbers (population of Himachal was then 1.3 million) and of peaceful nature, the people of Himachal were not considered much of a political force in the country. Realizing the hazards of the situation and the alternatives before them, the Pradesh leadership offered the supreme sacrifice and accepted the denial of democracy for retaining a separate entity for Himachal. On 31 October 1956, Himachal Vidhan Sabha was dissolved, the popular ministry handed over charge, and Himachal Pradesh became a union territory under an administrator designated as Lieutenant-Governor.

Politically and constitutionally it was a great setback for the Pradesh but its retention as a separate unit paid dividends in social and economic spheres in which advancement continued, though with retarded speed. The effects of socio-economic legislative measures, adopted during 1952-56, were being gradually realized. Besides, the spread of communications had brought people nearer to new ideas and they, by assimilating these, started gradually shedding their age-old isolation. Improvement of economy, specially in apple and seed-potato-growing areas, brought about a marked change in the attitudes of the people. Others getting the cue and inspiration from them started thinking and working on the same line. Nothing is so infectious as progress, once its practical fruits are visible. In Himachal the entire atmosphere was surcharged with new thinking and activity, only restricted by constitutional shackles by which it was tied up. The popular struggle for restoration of democracy continued in the traditional peaceful manner.

On 1 July 1963, the democratic set-up was restored in the Pradesh and its Territorial Council, which administered certain transferred subjects during the Lieutenant-Governor's rule, was converted into Legislative Assembly. The people, who had passed through a period of great agony for the last seven years, felt a great relief as their aspirations were realized. The political ferment of the years, thought not explosive, had left its mark on public feelings and behaviour. They were now more conscious of their rights which they zealously protected. Having lost centuries in ignorance and under unresponsive administrative set-ups, they were now extremely watchful and eager to avail of any opportunity of progress provided by their popular government. An era of self-help and through it self-confidence was in the making for the people.

The reorganization of Punjab in 1966, on linguistic basis, provided the hill areas of that state to forcefully voice their demand for integrating with Himachal Pradesh because of cultural, social, and linguistic similarities besides the similarity of the developmental problems. The wishes of the hill people in Himachal and Punjab were respected, and 1 November 1966 saw the integration of Himachal with Punjab hill areas comprising the districts of Kangra, Kullu, Lahaul and Spiti, and Simla, besides Nalagarh area of Ambala district, parts of Una tehsil of Hoshiarpur district and of Pathankot tehsil of Guradaspur district. With this integration the area of Himachal Pradesh increased to 55,658 sq. km., and it became bigger than that of the neighbouring states of Punjab and Haryana.

In view of the progress made by Himachal in various fields and the unanimous demand of its people, it was made a state of the Indian Union. Prime Minister Indira Gandhi inaugurated this eighteenth state of the country on 25 January 1971.

ECONOMIC DEVELOPMENT AND SOCIAL CHANGE

The unification of hill states under one administration set into motion various social, economic, and political forces which acting independently as also interacting helped to move the wheels of change faster than what could be ever imagined before. The constitution of Himachal Pradesh, as the first entirely hilly province of India, gave the hill people a new personality. Having found an identity, they started identifying their ills. Heart-searching started all over. What was true of political sphere found its corresponding beat in the economic and social fields as well. Huge gatherings being difficult in scarcely populated hilly terrains, the leaders of public opinion went from hamlet to hamlet explaining the significance of the new change, the meaning of which the people were themselves grasping with the disappearance of the feudal bureaucrats who had been a a terror to them.

The change also meant more social intercourse between the hill people as they were no longer restricted within the boundaries of their erstwhile states. Cultural unity was also realized more with the closeness of social contact. Marriage, customs, observances, functions, festivals, etc., which were to a great extent particular to each state area, crossed their erstwhile limits.

The initial years after the formation of Himachal Pradesh were utilized in providing a uniform administration. Different laws, administrative set-ups, and procedures were in vogue in different princely states and to bring about uniformity in them was not an easy task. Moreover, the struggle for democratization of its administration went on.

Till 1948, or even 1952, Himachal had only about 200 miles of roads and that too in isolated tracts. During the years of the first popular ministry top priority was given to road construction so much so that out of the total first plan expenditure of Rs 47.6 million in Himachal, Rs 24.5 million were spent on road construction alone. In 1956, motorable road length in Himachal was about 1,500 miles. Road construction actually spread out all over Himachal; on the one hand it provided employment to people while on the other it brought them in closer contact with the outside world as the communication lines started spreading. The centuries-old isolation of the hill people was disappearing.

Expansion of educational facilities through legislative and executive measures was another factor which helped people to do some rethinking about their old beliefs and prejudices. The first-ever educational survey was conducted in Himachal during 1955 which assessed the educational needs of all areas and spelled out a policy of opening primary, middle, and high schools looking to local terrain and the convenience of the students. The Himachal Pradesh Compulsory Primary Education Act was passed to focus the attention of people on the education of their children who were usually put on the job of grazing cattle and kine besides doing household chores. The results of the educational policy were astonishing so much so that literacy registered more than three-fold increase within a few years. In 1951, literacy was about 5 per cent while in 1961 it became 17.7 per cent, and now it is 31.32 per cent. Roads, which had suffered a comparative neglect during the second plan, were again awarded the highest priority while hydel generation on Himachal waters, which was so far left to other states, was taken up for the first time by the Pradesh government. Perennial rivers of Himachal are the highest source of power generation in northern India, but due to the constitutional position of Himachal, earlier as a Part "C" state and later as a union territory, projects like Bhakra (which has the second highest dam in the world) and Beas Sutlej Link, which were based on Himachal waters and located in its territory, were taken up for execution by the government of the neighbouring state of Punjab. In 1964, Himachal broke fresh ground in the field of hydel generation by opening its own Department of Multipurpose

Projects and Power and later by starting work on its first own multipurpose project, the Giri Bata Project.

By this time Himachal had established its name in the field of horticulture and it had come to be known as the "Apple State of India." Seeing the phenomenal prosperity of apple-growers, people living in similar agro-climatic conditions started taking after them. New lead was also provided to people living in lower altitudes to grow other suitable fruits such as peach, pear, plum, etc., which were no less profitable and which took lesser years to bear economically. Rapid expansion of horticulture helped in establishing subsidiary industries like packing-case-making and processing.

In the absence of road, Himachal forests had remained mostly unexploited or underexploited. A new regeneration policy for the forests was chalked out, besides new decisions on their scientific exploitation. Forest wealth had so far attracted only the forest contractor who had sold it as timber in the plains. Now the opening up of more forests besides availability of knowledge about the species of trees therein made it possible for the industrialists to think of starting forest-based industries in Himachal. As a result, a newsprint mill, a rayon-pulp factory, a chip-board factory, a high density carbon factory are now coming up in Himachal in the private sector besides various others that are in the processing stage. In the public sector a second rosin and turpentine factory was set up. Prior to this period, Himachal was never considered fit for setting up large, medium, or even small-scale industries and it was considered good enough for cottage industries only. But now the wind of change was blowing fast as one entrepreneur after another came forward with schemes to establish one unit or the other. The Himachal Pradesh Finance Corporation was set up for giving financial aid to the industrialists. This was besides the financial assistance provided by the Pradesh Industries Department.

Social and economic conditions, no doubt, determine the political life of a people to a great extent, but at the same time it is the proper use of political power that can serve as the most powerful instrument of social and economic change. Himachal had made great strides and traversed long distances in all directions—social, economic, and political—ever since it was created in 1948. Its people, while preserving their great cultural and social heritage, were fast adopting new scientific look on various problems. For example, they took to the idea of family planning more vigorously than most of the educated people in more advanced states of the Indian Union. The result has been that increase in population in Himachal Pradesh during 1961-1971 is 21.76 per cent as against the average of over 24 per cent.

During the tenure of the first popular ministry (24 March 1952 to 21 October 1956) the important socio-economic legislation adopted by Himachal included:

(1) H. P. Tenants Rights and Restoration Act.
(2) H. P. Debt Reduction Act.
(3) H. P. Abolition of Big Landed Estates and Land Reforms Act.
(4) The Punjab Tenancy (H. P. Amendment) Act.
(5) The Punjab Land Revenue (H. P. Amendment) Act.
(6) H. P. Land Revenue Act.
(7) H. P. Consolidation of Holdings and Prevention of Land Fragmentation Act.
(8) H. P. Land Development Act.
(9) H. P. Minor Canals Act.
(10) H. P. Bhoodan Yajna Act.
(11) H. P. Fruit Nurseries Act.
(12) H. P. Livestock Improvement Act.
(13) H. P. Panchayati Raj Act.
(14) H. P. Cooperative Societies Act.
(15) H. P. Private Forest Act.
(16) H. P. Water Supply Act.
(17) H. P. Language Act.
(18) H. P. Juvenile Prevention of Smoking Act.
(19) H. P. Compulsory Primary Education Act.
(20) H. P. Prevention of Ex-Communication Act.

After the integration of the parts of Punjab hills with

Himachal Pradesh in 1966, certain problems were faced, but these were not insurmountable. Gradually homogeneity was established and even the imaginary distinction of "old" and "new" areas disappeared. Laws, procedures, and taxes were made uniform and important legislative measures like the H. P. Transferred Territory Tenants Protection of Rights Act and its Amendment saved the tenants in the newly integrated areas from eviction. In old Himachal areas tenants had already security of tenure. Other important legislation affecting socio-economic life of the people of enlarged Pradesh were:

(1) H. P. Panchayat Raj Act.
(2) H. P. Cooperative Societies Act.
(3) H. P. Municipal Act.
(4) H. P. Urban Estate Development and Regulation Act.
(5) H. P. State Aid to Industries Act.
(6) H. P. Shops and Commercial Establishment Act.
(7) H. P. Industrial Establishment, National and Festival Holidays and Casual and Sick Leave Act.
(8) H. P. Water Supply Act.
(9) H. P. Agriculture Produce Market Act.
(10) H. P. Live-Stock and Bird Disease Act.
(11) H. P. Live-Stock Improvement Act.
(12) H. P. Agriculture Pest Diseases and Noxious Weeds Act.
(13) H. P. Capital of Himachal Pradesh Development and Regulation Act.
(14) H. P. Prohibition of Smoking (Show Houses) Act.
(15) H. P. Board of School Education Act.
(16) H. P. University Act.

All these measures, besides developmental schemes, intimately affected the life of the people. The income of Himachal as also of its people had registered a marked increase. The Pradesh Domestic income in 1971-72 (about Rs 300 million) has gone up by over 35 times as against Rs 8.5 million in 1948. Even during the recent years after the enlargement of Himachal, viz. 1967-68 to 1971-72, Himachal expenditure on economic development and social services has registered a steady increase, the highest being in the current years' proposals. The following table wil lgive an idea about this.

EXPENDITURE ON DEVELOPMENT SERVICE

(*Rs in millions*)

Year	Economic development	Social services	Total
1967-68	226.56	111.19	337.76
1968-69	295.54	118.10	413.65
1969-70	309.49	142.69	443.18
1970-71	299.91	170.65	470.55
1971-72	388.66	199.08	587.74

The headwise details of expenditure on economic development for 1967-68 and 1971-72 are as follows :

(*Rs in millions*)

Head of development	1967-68	1971-72	Percentage rise
Civil works	89.09	154.37	73.20
Forests	47.09	69.14	46.83
Road and water transport schemes	24.44	39.40	61.65
Agriculture	19.51	31.69	62.41
Animal husbandry	7.07	12.08	70.77
Electricity schemes	17.45	43.85	151.18
Industries	5.92	7.31	23.52
Cooperation	3.02	5.57	84.67
Others (Irrigation, C. D. projects, local development works)	12.94	25.23	94.97
Total	226.56	388.66	71.54

The per capita expenditure on development was Rs 172.20 in 1967-68 which rose to the tune of Rs 228.11 in 1971-72, registering an increase of 32.5 per cent. Similarly, the per capita expenditure incurred in the budget of 1971-72 on education and medical and public health was Rs 36.76 and Rs 11.79 respectively as against Rs 21.69 and Rs 8.54 during 1967-68. As a result of increase in the expenditure on development the per capita income at current prices has risen from Rs 240 in 1950-51 to Rs 493 in 1968-69.

I may as well refer to very important sociological changes that have come about amongst the people in the areas which were affected by polyandry. As pointed out earlier there have been immense changes not only in the matter of marital relations or social institutions but great economic, development, administrative, and political activities have also immensely transformed the whole structure of society and economic and social conditions of the people. As such it is very necessary to note how the economic transformation has had its impact not only on the social institutions and marital relations but on the disintegration of caste barriers, the relationship of landlords and tenants, and the breaking-up of feudalism. The institution of Reet which had caused deep concern has undergone a great change. With the abolition of Reet tax by Sirmur state and the freedom of people from the princely bondage after Suket Satyagraha, the whole picture regarding Reet has changed. Even though the divorces and remarriages continue, the monetary consideration which had formed the basis of this custom in the past has practically disappeared. A new consciousness has consequently grown up for a proper family life. In no other field has the effect of independence and the formation of a new state on the people of the hills has been more evident than in this new relationship and a complete break from the past. Not that divorce and remarriage have stopped but they are resorted to only when necessary and that too without monetary consideration.

POLYANDRY

In the matter of practising of polyandry again certain very important changes have taken place and a new society has emerged. Polyandry has little trace now in Sirmur district excepting for the two areas known as Kangra and Mahal Bhojes where it is still practised though in a different form of Jori-dari. In Jori-dari it is only two brothers who have a common wife and if there are more than one the others too have one wife for every two. Even that is disappearing and this is so in spite of the fact that the disparity between the proportion of sexes still continues as the following chart of the census of 1961 will show:

Name of Bhoj	Name of Tehsil/Sub-Tehsil	Name of Patwar Circles	Population			Population per thousand	
			Male	Female	Total	Male	Female
MAHAL	Reinka	Tikridasakna	1,042	764	1,806	1,363	733
	Shillai	Barol	1,701	1,530	3,231	1,111	899
		Panog	1,346	1,051	2,397	1,280	787
		Sangna	1,782	1,328	3,060	1,378	766
		Total Mahal	5,821	4,673	10,494	1,246	802
KANGRA	Reinka	Nainidhar	1,914	1,551	3,465	1,234	810
	Shillai	Bandli	1,574	1,361	2,935	1,156	801
		Shillai	2,168	1,527	3,695	1,419	704
		Gawali	2,135	1,638	3,773	1,303	767
		Total	7,791	6,077	13.868	1,282	780
	Paonta	Mashu	1,706	1,319	3,025	1,293	767
		Dogana	1,885	1,507	3,392	1,250	799
		Tatiana	1,483	1,126	2,609	1,317	758
		Total	5,074	3,952	9,026	1,284	778
GRAND TOTAL		Kangra (Distt. Sirmur)	12,865	10,029	22,894	1,282	779

While the proportion of sexes has not very much changed and the desire to leave an estate undivided is still there and land has not increased, the custom has undergone a great change due to the construction of roads, economic prosperity, educational facilities, and employment opportunities. Economic forces have counter-balanced all propaganda and even religious and social considerations.

In most of the other areas also polyandry is losing its hold, as in Sirmur, and I am glad the transformation has come about much sooner than expected due to the great economic transformation. The women in these hills today enjoy a status and hold a position in society which would be the envy of most modern sophisticated women in the plains and their contribution to the progress and prosperity of the society has been in no way less than that of men.

What were considered to be the most inaccessible areas have today been opened to vehicular traffic, sometimes passing over heights of 12,000 to 15,000 feet. Motorable roads go right up to the borders of Tibet both near Shipkila, Kaurik and

Lahaul has been connected to Ladakh, being the highest road in the world. The roads, built by hard work and labour, have brought new light and productive activity. The name of the late S.N. Stokes, an American social worker who later decided to settle at Kotgarh and embraced Hinduism, would ever be cherished in the history of Himachal as he brought about a great economic revolution by introducing delicious varieties of apples from America with the help of latest scientific researches and modern practices of apple-growing.

With the enactment of the Abolition of Big Landed Estates and Land Reforms Act in the Himachal Pradesh Act (1954) the whole picture of relationship between the landlord and tenants, besides the condition of the peasantry, has undergone a great transformation. According to the old laws, it was only the occupancy tenants whose tenancy was secured. The non-occupancy tenants and those holding lands under contracts or leases had no security of any type. By the above-stated enactment of 1954, both the occupancy tenants including the lease or contract-holders were enabled to become proprietors of lands under their cultivation.

The old system of the *begar*, i.e. forced labour without payment, has been abolished and any extra hands engaged on the farm receive wages in kind and cash.

Today the picture which these hills present is absolutely different from what it was before independence. All this has had a great effect on the whole social structure. In those days none but Bhats, Dewas, and Kanets could enter a temple. Kolis or any other so-called low caste could not drink at the source with Bhats and Kanets. Then only those who belonged to the ruling house generally called themselves Rajputs, the other were ordinarily called Kanets. All this has changed. Kanets are not only now fully recognized as Rajputs as was decided by the Punjab Government long time ago but some of them even consider themselves superior to Rajputs for according to them they alone have kept up their blue blood. The progressive section of Kolis now call themselves Rajputs and have adopted the Gotras of the latter. While the older generation does not like it, the young generation has accepted it and so these social barriers have been removed very greatly.

With the spread of education practically in all the areas and opening of service avenues for both boys and girls, there has been a much greater social mixing and quite a number of inter-community and inter-caste marriages have taken place which have further broken down these barriers of castes and community.

The artificial condition or stigmas attached to the various communities which were considered inferior have been greatly removed and this has resulted in an immense social change. The distinction between Rajputs or Kanets, Bhats or Brahmins has practically disappeared and Kanets are taken to be as good as Rajputs and Bhats as good as Brahmins. Kolis, who too were treated with contempt, found a new status, equivalent to that of the Rajputs and the Brahmins. The social disqualifications attached to any community have been removed. In fact, the differences between different communities have disappeared to a great extent except in certain pockets in inaccessible areas. With the reservation of seats for the scheduled castes and tribes like Kolis, Dumnas, Chamars, etc. in the Panchayats, the Municipal Committees, the Legislative Assembly, Parliament, and in the services they have found a proper status of which they had been deprived of for ages. The status today in fact is determined more by the economic or political position of an individual or family than by the caste or community to which one belongs.

The changes have been mentioned to give an idea of the transformation that has taken place in sociological, economic, and administrative set-up in these hills after the attainment of independence and introduction of democratic institutions, besides the launching of development activities under the five-year plans which has been one of the most valuable and lasting contributions of the late Prime Minister Jawaharlal Nehru and the present Prime Minister Indira Gandhi.

This, in brief, is the changing socio-economic and political picture of Himachal Pradesh.

INDEX

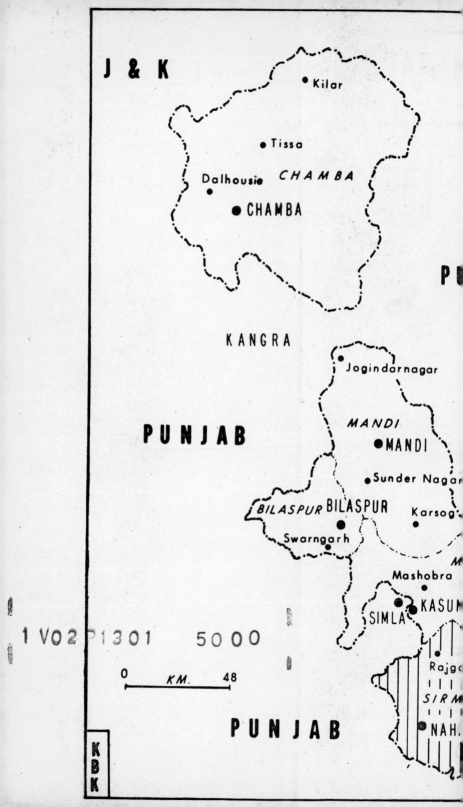